THE
NATURE
OF
CALIFORNIA

AN INTRODUCTION TO COMMON PLANTS AND ANIMALS AND NATURAL ATTRACTIONS

Series Created and Edited by James Kavanagh

Illustrations by Raymond Leung

Introduction by James C. Rettie

WATERFORD PRESS

Reviews for *The Nature of California:*

"The Nature of California offers an agreeable overview of animals and plants casual hikers and campers are likely to encounter . . . a useful book to keep with the picnic supplies or camping gear."

LA Times

"With so many detailed guides in print, it would be tempting to overlook this book, yet it fills a valuable niche. Small and light, [it features] lovely color illustrations of several hundred species of plants, mammals, reptiles, fish and birds."

San Francisco Chronicle

"A useful and informative guide . . . this is a user-friendly book with an excellent introduction."

Books of the Southwest Review

"A colorful paperback field guide for people of all ages."

California Biodiversity News

CONTENTS

Publisher's Cataloguing in Publication Data
Kavanagh, James Daniel, 1960-
The Nature of California. An Introduction to Common Plants and Animals and Natural Attractions. Includes bibliographical references and index.
1. Natural History – California. 2. Animals–Identification–California.
3. Plants–Identification–California. 4. Tourism–California.

Library of Congress Catalogue Card Number: 96-61161
ISBN: 0-9640225-4-0

Distributed to the trade in North America by Falcon Press, P.O. Box 1716, Helena, MT 59624. Phone (800) 582-2665.

The introductory essay, "BUT A WATCH IN THE NIGHT" by JAMES C. RETTIE is from FOREVER THE LAND by RUSSELL AND KATE LORD. Copyright © 1950 by Harper and Brothers, renewed copyright © 1978 by Russell and Kate Lord. Reprinted with permission of HarperCollins Publishers.

Illustrator   Raymond Leung
Consultants   William E. Grenfell Jr., H. William Lunt Ph. D, Ken McKowen, Judson Vandevere, Maury Solomon.

While every attempt has been made to ensure the accuracy of the information in this guide, it is important to note that experts often disagree with one another regarding the common name, size, appearance, habitat and distribution of species. The publisher welcomes all comments and suggestions.

Printed in Hong Kong.

To Jill

PREFACE

THE NATURE OF CALIFORNIA is intended to highlight the state's common and distinctive species of plants and animals and its outstanding natural attractions.

This guide's primary purpose is to introduce the reader to familiar plants and animals and highlight the diversity of species found in California. Its secondary purpose is to show how all species in each ecosystem found here depend on each other, directly and indirectly, for survival.

The guide opens with a brief introduction to evolution in order to highlight the similarities and differences between major groups of plants and animals and show when each appeared in geologic time. The brilliant introductory essay by James C. Rettie provides a simplified view of the evolution of life on earth, and the role that man – the animal – has played to date.

I am indebted to dozens of helpful people who assisted me in the monumental task of researching and writing this guide, including staff at the California Department of Parks and Recreation, the California Department of Fish and Game, the US Fish and Wildlife Service, the California Office of Tourism, the Boy Scouts and Girl Scouts of America and the California Academy of Sciences. I would like to thank my critics at these organizations and other experts who reviewed an early draft of the guide and contributed hundreds of valuable comments and criticisms.

J.D.K.

BUT A WATCH IN THE NIGHT

BY JAMES C. RETTIE

James C. Rettie wrote the following essay while working for the National Forest Service in 1948. In a flash of brilliance, he converted the statistics from an existing government pamphlet on soil erosion into an analogy for the ages.

OUT BEYOND OUR SOLAR SYSTEM there is a planet called Copernicus. It came into existence some four or five billion years before the birth of our earth. In due course of time it became inhabited by a race of intelligent men.

About 750 million years ago the Copernicans had developed the motion picture machine to a point well in advance of the stage that we have reached. Most of the cameras that we now use in motion picture work are geared to take twenty-four pictures per second on a continuous strip of film. When such film is run through a projector, it throws a series of images on the screen and these change with a rapidity that gives the visual impression of normal movement. If a motion is too swift for the human eye to see it in detail, it can be captured and artificially slowed down by means of the slow-motion camera. This one is geared to take many more shots per second – ninety-six or even more than that. When the slow motion film is projected at the normal speed of twenty-four pictures per second, we can see just how the jumping horse goes over a hurdle.

What about motion that is too slow to be seen by the human eye? That problem has been solved by the use of the time-lapse camera. In this one, the shutter is geared to take only one shot per second, or one per minute, or even one per hour – depending upon the kind of movement that is being photographed. When the time-lapse film is projected at the normal speed of twenty-four pictures per second, it is possible to see a bean sprout growing up out of the ground. Time-lapse films are useful in the study of many types of motion too slow to be observed by the unaided, human eye.

The Copernicans, it seems, had time-lapse cameras some 757 million years ago and they also had superpowered telescopes that gave them a clear view of what was happening upon this earth. They decided to make a film record of the life history of earth and to make it on the scale of one picture per year. The photography has been in progress during the last 757 million years.

In the near future, a Copernican interstellar expedition will arrive upon our earth and bring with it a copy of the time-lapse film. Arrangements will be made for showing the entire film in one continuous run. This will begin at midnight of New Year's eve and continue day and night without a single stop until midnight on December 31. The rate of projection will be 24 pictures per second. Time on the screen will thus seem to move at the rate of twenty-four years per second; 1440 years per minute; 86,400 years per hour; approximately two million years per day and sixty-two million years per month. The normal lifespan of individual man will occupy about three seconds. The full period of earth history that will be unfolded on the screen (some 757 million years) will extend from what the geologists call the Pre-Cambrian times up to the present. This will, by no means, cover the full time-span of the earth's geological history but it will embrace the period since the advent of living organisms.

During the months of January, February, and March the picture will be desolate and dreary. The shape of the land masses and the oceans will bear little or no resemblance to those that we know. The violence of geological erosion will be much in evidence. Rains will pour down on the land and promptly go booming down to the seas. There will be no clear streams anywhere except where the rains fall upon hard rock. Everywhere on the steeper ground the stream channels will be filled with boulders hurled down by rushing waters. Raging torrents and dry stream beds will keep alternating in quick succession. High mountains will seem to melt like so much butter in the sun. The shifting of land into the seas, later to be thrust up as new mountains, will be going on at a grand scale.

Early in April there will be some indication of the presence of single-celled living organisms in some of the warmer and sheltered coastal waters. By the end of the month it will be noticed that some of these organisms have become multicellular. A few of them, including the Trilobites, will be encased in hard shells.

Toward the end of May, the first vertebrates will appear, but they will still be aquatic creatures. In June about 60 per cent of the land area that we know as North America will be under water. One broad channel will occupy the space where the Rocky Mountains now stand. Great deposits of limestone will be forming under some of the shallower seas. Oil and gas deposits will be in process of formation – also under shallow seas. On land there will be no sign of vegetation. Erosion will be rampant, tearing loose particles and chunks of rock and grinding them into sand and silt to be spewed out by the streams into bays and estuaries.

About the middle of July the first land plants will appear and take up the tremendous job of soil building. Slowly, very slowly, the mat of vegetation will spread, always battling for its life against the power of erosion. Almost foot by foot, the plant life will advance, lacing down with its root structures whatever pulverized rock material it can find. Leaves and stems will be giving added protection against the loss of the soil foothold. The increasing vegetation will pave the way for the land animals that will live upon it.

Early in August the seas will be teeming with fish. This will be what geologists call the Devonian period. Some of the races of these fish will be breathing by means of lung tissue instead of through gill tissues. Before the month is over, some of the lung fish will go ashore and take on a crude lizard-like appearance. Here are the first amphibians.

In early September the insects will put in their appearance. Some will look like huge dragonflies and will have a wing span of 24 inches. Large portions of the land masses will now be covered with heavy vegetation that will include the primitive spore-propagating trees. Layer upon layer of this plant growth will build up, later to appear as coal deposits. About the middle of this month, there will be evidence of the first seed-bearing plants and the first reptiles. Heretofore, the land animals will have been amphibians that could reproduce their kind only by depositing a soft egg mass in quiet waters. The reptiles will be shown to be freed from the aquatic bond because they can reproduce by means of a shelled egg in which the embryo and its nurturing liquids are sealed and thus protected from destructive evaporation. Before September is over, the first dinosaurs will be seen – creatures destined to dominate the animal realm for about 140 million years and then to disappear.

In October there will be series of mountain uplifts along what is now the eastern coast of the United States. A creature with feathered limbs - half bird and half reptile in appearance – will take itself into the air. Some small and rather unpretentious animals will be seen to bring forth their young in a form that is a miniature replica of the parents and to feed these young on milk secreted by mammary glands in the female parent. The emergence of this mammalian form of animal life will be recognized as one of the great events in geologic time. October will also witness the high-water mark of the dinosaurs – creatures ranging in size from that of the modern goat to monsters like Brontosaurus that weighed some 40 tons. Most of them will be placid vegetarians, but a few will be hideous-looking carnivores, like Allosaurus and Tyrannosaurus. Some of the herbivorous dinosaurs will be clad in bony armor for protection against their flesh-eating comrades.

November will bring pictures of a sea extending from the Gulf of Mexico to the Arctic in space now occupied by the Rocky Mountains. A few of the reptiles will take to the air on bat-like wings. One of these, called Pteranodon, will have a wingspread of 15 feet. There will be a rapid development of the modern flowering plants, modern trees, and modern insects. The dinosaurs will disappear. Toward the end of the month there will be a tremendous land disturbance in which the Rocky Mountains will rise out of the sea to assume a dominating place in the North American landscape.

As the picture runs on into December it will show the mammals in command of the animal life. Seed-bearing trees and grasses will have covered most of the land with a heavy mantle of vegetation. Only the areas newly thrust up from the sea will be barren. Most of the streams will be crystal clear. The turmoil of geological erosion will be confined to localized areas. About December 25 will begin the cutting of the Grand Canyon of the Colorado River. Grinding down through layer after layer of sedimentary strata, this stream will finally expose deposits laid down in Pre-Cambrian times. Thus in the walls of that canyon will appear geological formations dating from recent times to the period when the earth had no living organisms upon it.

The picture will run on through the latter days of December and even up to its final day with still no sign of mankind. The spectators will become alarmed in the fear that man has somehow been left out. But not so; sometime about noon on December 31 (one million years ago) will appear a stooped, massive creature of man-like proportions. This will be Pithecanthropus, the Java ape man. For tools and weapons he will have nothing but crude stone and wooden clubs. His children will live a precarious existence threatened on the one side by hostile animals and on the other by tremendous climatic changes. Ice sheets – in places 4,000 feet deep – will form in the northern parts of North America and Eurasia. Four times this glacial ice will push southward to cover half the continents. With each advance the plant and animal life will be swept under or pushed southward. With each recession of the ice, life will struggle to reestablish itself in the wake of the retreating glaciers. The woolly mammoth, the musk ox, and the caribou all will fight to maintain themselves near the ice line. Sometimes they will be caught and put into cold storage – skin, flesh, blood, bones, and all.

The picture will run on through supper time with still very little evidence of man's presence on earth. It will be about 11 o'clock when Neanderthal man appears. Another half hour will go by before the appearance of Cro-Magnon man living in caves and painting crude animal pictures on the walls of his dwelling. Fifteen minutes more will bring Neolithic man, knowing how to chip stone and thus produce sharp cutting edges for spears and tools. In a few minutes more it will appear that man has domesticated the dog, the sheep and, possibly, other animals. He will then begin the use of milk. He will also learn the arts of basket weaving and the making of pottery and dugout canoes.

The dawn of civilization will not come until about five or six minutes before the end of the picture. The story of the Egyptians, the Babylonians, the Greeks, and the Romans will unroll during the fourth, the third, and the second minute before the end. At 58 minutes and 43 seconds past 11:00 P.M. (just 1 minute and 17 seconds before the end) will come the beginning of the Christian era. Columbus will discover the new world 20 seconds before the end. The Declaration of Independence will be signed just 7 seconds before the final curtain comes down.

In those few moments of geologic time will be the story of all that has happened since we became a nation. And what a story it will be! A human swarm will sweep across the face of the continent and take it away from the red men (*sic*). They will change it far more radically than it has ever been changed before in a comparable time. The great virgin forests will be seen going down before ax and fire. The soil, covered for eons by its protective mantle of trees and grasses, will be laid bare to the ravages of water and wind erosion. Streams that had been flowing clear will, once again, take up a load of silt and push it toward the seas. Humus and mineral salts, both vital elements of productive soil, will be seen to vanish at a terrifying rate. The railroads and highways and cities that will spring up may divert attention, but they cannot cover up the blight of man's recent activities. In great sections of Asia, it will be seen that man must utilize cow dung and every scrap of available straw or grass for fuel to cook his food. The forests that once provided wood for this purpose will be gone without a trace. The use of these agricultural wastes for fuel, in place of returning them to the land, will be leading to increasing soil impoverishment. Here and there will be seen a dust storm darkening the landscape over an area a thousand miles across. Man-creatures will be shown counting their wealth in terms of bits of printed paper representing other bits of a scarce but comparatively useless yellow metal that is kept buried in strong vaults. Meanwhile, the soil, the only real wealth that can keep mankind alive on the face of this earth is savagely being cut loose from its ancient moorings and washed into the seven seas.

We have just arrived upon this earth. How long will we stay ?

This guide describes more than 325 species of plants and animals that are common in California. The term 'common' is intended to refer to those species which are abundant, widely distributed and easy to observe in the field. A few less common and more localized species have also been included to provide readers with insight into the diversity of organisms found in California.

Throughout the book, plants and animals are arranged more-or-less in their taxonomic groupings. Exceptions have been made when non-traditional groupings facilitate field identification for the novice (e.g., wildflowers are grouped by color).

Because this guide has been written for the novice, every attempt has been made to simplify presentation of the material. Illustrations are accompanied by brief descriptions of key features, and technical terms have been held to a minimum throughout.

SPECIES TEXT

The species descriptions has been fragmented to simplify presentation of material:

ARROWHEAD
The name in bold type indicates the common name of the species. It is important to note that a single species may have many common names. The above plant is also commonly called 'Wapato' and 'Tule Potato.'

Sagittaria latifolia
The italicized latin words refer to an organism's scientific name, a universally accepted two-part term that precisely defines its relationship to other organisms. The first capitalized word, the genus, refers to groups of closely related organisms. The second term, the species name, refers to organisms that look similar and interbreed freely. If the second word in the term is '*spp.*', this indicates there are several species in the genus that look similar to the one illustrated. If a third word appears in the term, it identifies a subspecies, a group of individuals that are even more closely related.

Size
Generally indicates the average length of animals (nose to tail tip) and the average height of plants. Exceptions are noted in the text.

Description
Key markings and/or characteristics that help to distinguish one species from another.

Habitat
> Where a species lives/can be found.

Comments
> General information regarding distinctive behaviors, diet, related species, etc.

ILLUSTRATIONS

The majority of animal illustrations show the adult male in its breeding coloration. Plant illustrations are designed to highlight the characteristics that are most conspicuous in the field. It is important to note that coloration, size and shape may vary depending on age, sex and season.

CHECKLISTS

The checklists are provided to allow you to keep track of the plants and animals you identify.

TIPS ON FIELD IDENTIFICATION

Identifying a species in the field can be as simple as one-two-three:

1. Note key markings, characteristics and/or behaviors;
2. Find an illustration that matches; and
3. Read the text to confirm your sighting.

Identifying mammals or birds in the field is not fundamentally different than identifying trees, flowers or other forms of life. It is simply a matter of knowing what to look for. Reading the introductory text to each section will make you aware of key characteristics of each group and allow you to use the guide more effectively in the field.

N.B. – We refer primarily to common species in this guide and do not list all species within any group. The references listed in the back of this guide are intended for those who would like more detailed information about a specific area of study.

EVOLUTION OF ANIMALS

WHAT IS AN ANIMAL?

Animals are living organisms which can generally be distinguished from plants in four ways:
  1) they feed on plants and other animals;
  2) they have a nervous system;
  3) they can move freely and are not rooted; and
  4) their cells do not have rigid walls or contain chlorophyll.

All animals are members of the animal kingdom, a group consisting of over a million species. Species are classified within the animal kingdom according to their evolutionary relationships to one another.

Most of the animals discussed in this guide are members of the group called vertebrates. They all possess backbones and most have complex brains and highly developed senses.

The earliest vertebrates arose in the oceans about 500 million years ago. Today, surviving species are divided into five main groups.

- Fishes
- Amphibians
- Reptiles
- Birds
- Mammals

Following is a simplified description of the evolution of the vertebrates and the differences between groups.

FISHES

The oldest form of vertebrate life, fishes evolved from invertebrate sea creatures 400-500 million years ago. All are cold-blooded (ectothermic) and their activity levels are largely influenced by the surrounding environment.

The first species were armored and jawless and fed by filtering tiny organisms from water and mud. Surviving members of this group include lampreys and hagfishes. Jawless fishes were succeeded by jawed fishes that quickly came to dominate the seas, and still do today. The major surviving groups include:

  1) Sharks and rays – more primitive species which possess soft skeletons made of cartilage; and
  2) Bony fishes – a more recent and better-known group of fishes which comprise most of the surviving species.

Physiological Characteristics of Fishes

Heart and gills

A two-chambered heart circulates the blood through a simple system of arteries and veins. Gills act like lungs and allow fish to absorb dissolved oxygen from the water into their bloodstream.

Nervous system

Small anterior brain is connected to a spinal cord which runs the length of the body.

Digestive system

Digestive system is complete. A number of specialized organs produce enzymes which help to break down food in the stomach and intestines. Kidneys extract urine from the blood and wastes are eliminated through the anus.

Reproduction

In most fishes, the female lays numerous eggs in water and the male fertilizes them externally. Young hatch as larvae, and the larval period ranges from a few hours to several years. Survival rate of young is low.

Senses

Most have the senses of taste, touch, smell, hearing and sight, though their vision is poor. Fishes hear and feel by sensing vibrations and temperature and pressure changes in the surrounding water.

AMPHIBIANS

The first limbed land-dwellers, amphibians evolved from fishes 300-400 million years ago and became the dominant land vertebrates for over 100 million years. Like fishes, amphibians are cold-blooded and their activity levels are largely influenced by the environment.

Some believe that the first amphibians arose because of the intense competition for survival in the water. The first fish-like amphibian ancestors to escape the water were those that had the ability to breathe air and possessed strong, paired fins that allowed them to wriggle onto mud-flats and sandbars. (Living relics of this group include five species of lungfish and the rare coelacanth.) Though amphibians were able to exploit rich new habitats on land, they remained largely dependent on aquatic environments for survival and reproduction.

The major surviving groups are:

1) Salamanders – slender-bodied, short-legged, long-tailed creatures that live secretive lives in dark, damp areas; and
2) Frogs and toads – squat-bodied, amphibians with long hind legs, large heads and large eyes, they are common residents of rural and urban ponds and lakes.

Advances Made Over Fishes

Lungs and legs

> By developing lungs and legs, amphibians freed themselves from the competition for food in aquatic environments and were able to flourish as a group on land.

Improved circulatory system

> Amphibians evolved a heart with three chambers that enhanced gas exchange in the lungs and provided body tissues with highly oxygenated blood.

Ears

> Frogs and toads developed external ears that enhanced their listening ability, an essential adaptation for surviving on land.

Reproduction

> Most amphibians reproduce like fish, though salamanders differ in that most fertilize eggs internally rather than externally; in many, the male produces a sperm packet which the female collects and uses to fertilize eggs as they are laid.

REPTILES

Reptiles first appeared 300-350 million years ago. They soon came to dominate the earth, and continued to rule the land, sea and air for over 130 million years. Cold-blooded like amphibians, reptiles evolved a host of characteristics that made them better suited for life on land.

About 65 million years ago, the dominant reptiles mysteriously underwent a mass extinction. A popular theory suggests this was caused by a giant meteor hitting the earth which sent up a huge dust cloud that blocked out the sun's light and caused temperatures to drop and plants to die off.

The major surviving reptilian groups are:

1) Turtles – hard-shelled reptiles with short legs;
2) Lizards – scaly-skinned reptiles with long legs and tails;
3) Snakes – long, legless reptiles with scaly skin; and
4) Crocodilians – very large reptiles with elongate snouts, toothy jaws and long tails.

Advances Made Over Amphibians

Reproduction

> Fertilization is by copulation and females lay leathery, shelled eggs. The development of the shelled egg was the single most important evolutionary advancement for the group since this freed them from dependence on a watery environment and allowed them to exploit new habitats on land unchallenged. The young did not go through a larval stage and were independent from birth.

Dry, scaly skin
> Their dry skin prevented water loss and also protected them from predators.

Posture
> Many reptiles evolved an upright posture and strong legs which enhanced their mobility on land.

Improved heart and lungs
> Their heart and lungs were more efficient, allowing them to be more active. The heart had four chambers (though the division between ventricles was usually incomplete).

Defense
> They were agile and better able to defend themselves, having sharp claws and teeth or beaks capable of inflicting wounds.

BIRDS

Birds evolved from reptiles 100-200 million years ago. Unlike species before them, birds were warm-blooded (endothermic) and able to regulate their body temperature internally.* This meant that they could maintain high activity levels despite fluctuations in environmental temperature. They are believed to have evolved from a group of gliding reptiles, with their scaly legs considered proof of their reptilian heritage.

*There is still a debate over whether or not some dinosaurs were warm-blooded.

Advances Made Over Reptiles

Ability to fly
> By evolving flight, birds were able to exploit environments that were inaccessible to their competitors and predators. The characteristics they evolved that allowed them to fly included wings, feathers, hollow bones, an enhanced breathing capacity and a true four-chambered heart.

Warm-blooded
> An insulating layer of feathers enhanced their capacity to retain heat. They also had completely four-chambered hearts.

Keen senses
> Birds evolved very keen senses of vision and hearing and developed complex behavioral and communicative patterns.

Reproduction
> Fertilization is internal and the eggs have hard, rather than leathery, shells. Unlike most reptiles, birds incubate their eggs themselves and protect and nurture their young for a period following birth.

MAMMALS

Mammals evolved from reptiles 100-200 million years ago. Though warm-blooded like birds, they are believed to have different reptilian ancestors. In addition to being warm-blooded, mammals also evolved physiological adaptations which allowed them to hunt prey and avoid predation better than their competition.

Mammals quickly came to exploit the habitats left vacant by dinosaurs and have been the dominant land vertebrates for the past 65 million years. Man is a relatively new addition to the group, having a lineage less than three million years old.

Mammals have evolved into three distinct groups, all of which have living representatives:

1) <u>Monotremes</u> – egg-laying mammals (the platypus and echidna);
2) <u>Marsupials</u> – pouched mammals which bear living, embryonic young; and
3) <u>Placentals</u> – mammals which bear fully-developed young.

Advances Made Over Birds

<u>Reproduction</u>

Fertilization is internal but in most the young develop in the female's uterus instead of an egg. After birth, the young are fed and nurtured by adults for an extensive period, during which they learn behavioral lessons from their elders and siblings. This emphasis on learned responses at an early age is believed to contribute to the superior intelligence and reproductive success of the group.

<u>Hearing</u>

Most have three bones in the middle ear to enhance hearing. (Birds and reptiles have one.)

<u>Teeth</u>

Many developed specialized teeth that allowed them to rely on a variety of food sources. Incisors were for cutting, canines for tearing and molars for chewing or shearing.

<u>Breathing</u>

Mammals evolved a diaphragm which increases breathing efficiency.

<u>Posture</u>

Many have long, strong legs and are very agile on land.

EVOLUTION OF PLANTS

WHAT IS A PLANT?

Plants are living organisms which can generally be distinguished from animals in four ways:

1) They synthesize their own food from carbon dioxide, water and sunlight;
2) They do not have a nervous system;
3) Most are rooted and cannot move around easily; and
4) Their cells have rigid walls and contain chlorophyll, a pigment needed for photosynthesis.

All plants are members of the plant kingdom. According to the fossil record, plants evolved from algae that originated nearly three billion years ago. Since then, plants have evolved into millions of species in a mind-boggling assortment of groups.

Because plant classification is exceedingly complex, we will limit our review to two groups which encompass many of the most familiar plants, namely:

1) Gymnosperms – plants with naked seeds;
2) Angiosperms – flowering plants with enclosed seeds.

GYMNOSPERMS – THE NAKED SEED PLANTS

This group of mostly evergreen trees and shrubs includes some of the largest and oldest known plants. They began to appear around 300-400 million years ago, and were the dominant plant species on earth for nearly 200 million years. The most successful surviving group of gymnosperms are the conifers, which include such species as pines, spruces, firs, larches and junipers.

Most conifers are evergreen and have small needle-like or scale-like leaves which are adapted to withstand extreme temperature changes. Some species are deciduous, but most retain their leaves for two or more years before shedding them.

Reproduction

Most evergreens produce woody 'cones'– conical fruits that contain the male and female gametes. The male cones produce pollen that is carried by the wind to settle between the scales of female cones on other trees. The pollen stimulates ovules to change into seeds, and the scales of the female cone close up to protect the seeds. When the seeds are ripe – up to two years later – environmental conditions stimulate the cone to open its scales and the naked seeds fall to the ground.

ANGIOSPERMS – THE FLOWERING PLANTS

Angiosperms first appeared in the fossil record around 130 million years ago. They quickly adapted to a wide variety of environments, and by the Cretaceous Period had succeeded gymnosperms as the dominant land plants. Their reproductive success was largely due to two key adaptations:

1) They produced flowers which attracted pollinating agents such as insects and birds; and
2) They produced seeds encased in 'fruits', to aid in seed dispersal.

Angiosperms make up a diverse and widespread group of plants ranging from trees and shrubs such as oaks, cherries, maples, hazelnuts, and apples, to the more typical flowers like lilies, orchids, roses, daisies, and violets. The trees and shrubs within this group are commonly referred to as 'deciduous', and most shed their leaves annually.

Reproduction

A typical flower has colorful petals that encircle the male and female reproductive structures (see illustration in introduction to wildflowers). The male stamens are composed of thin filaments supporting anthers containing pollen. The female pistil contains unfertilized seeds in the swollen basal part called the ovary. Pollination occurs when pollen — carried by the wind or animals — reaches the pistil.

Once fertilization has occurred, the ovules develop into seeds and the ovary into a fruit. The fruit and seeds mature together, with the fruit ripening to the point where the seeds are capable of germinating. At maturity, each seed contains an embryo and a food supply to nourish it upon germination. Upon ripening, the fruit may fall to the ground with the seeds still inside it, as in peaches, cherries, and squash, or it may burst open and scatter its seeds in the wind, like poplar trees, willows, and dandelions.

Fruit comes in many forms, from grapes, tomatoes, apples, and pears, to pea and bean pods, nuts, burrs and capsules. Regardless of the shape it takes, fruit enhances the reproductive success of angiosperms in two important ways. First, it helps to protect the seeds from the elements until they have fully matured, enabling them to survive unfavorable conditions. Secondly, fruit aids in seed dispersal. Some fruits are eaten by animals that eventually release the seeds in their feces, an ideal growing medium. Others may be spiny or burred so they catch on the coats of animals, or may have special features which enable them to be carried away from their parent plant by the wind or water.

GEOLOGICAL TIMESCALE

ERA	PERIOD	MYA*	EVENTS
CENOZOIC	HOLOCENE	.01	Dominance of man.
CENOZOIC	QUATERNARY	2.5	First human civilizations.
CENOZOIC	TERTIARY	65	Mammals, birds, insects and angiosperms dominate the land.
MESOZOIC	CRETACEOUS	135	Dinosaurs extinct. Mammals, insects and angiosperms undergo great expansion. Gymnosperms decline.
MESOZOIC	JURASSIC	190	Age of Reptiles; dinosaurs dominant. First birds appear.
MESOZOIC	TRIASSIC	225	First dinosaurs and mammals appear. Gymnosperms are dominant plants.
PALEOZOIC	PERMIAN	280	Great expansion of reptiles causes amphibians to decline. Many marine invertebrates become extinct.
PALEOZOIC	CARBONIFEROUS	340	Age of Amphibians; amphibians dominant. First reptiles appear. Fish undergo a great expansion.
PALEOZOIC	DEVONIAN	400	Age of Fishes; fishes dominant. First amphibians, insects and gymnosperms appear.
PALEOZOIC	SILURIAN	430	First jawed fishes appear. Plants move onto land.
PALEOZOIC	ORDOVICIAN	500	First vertebrates appear.
PALEOZOIC	CAMBRIAN	600	Marine invertebrates and algae abundant.

*Millions of years ago

WHAT ARE MAMMALS?

Most mammals are warm-blooded, furred creatures that have four feet and a tail, five digits on each foot, and several different kinds of teeth. All North American species give birth to live young which are fed on milk from their mother's mammary glands.

HOW TO IDENTIFY MAMMALS

Mammals are generally secretive in their habits and therefore difficult to spot in the field. Some of the best places to look for them are in undisturbed areas affording some source of cover including woods and wood edges, swamps, thickets, and rural fields and meadows.

When you spot a mammal, consider its size, shape, and color. Check for distinguishing field marks and note the surrounding habitat.

COMMON TRACKS

Studying tracks is an easy way to discover the kinds of mammals found in your area. For more information on animal tracks, see the references under mammals on page 168.

Mouse Jackrabbit Skunk Squirrel

Dog Cat Marmot Opossum

Elk Sheep Deer (dew claws) Bear

N.B. – Tracks are not to scale

MARSUPIALS

Related to kangaroos and koalas, the opossum is the only marsupial found in North America. Young are born prematurely and move to a fur-lined pouch (marsupium) where they complete their development attached to a teat.

OPOSSUM
Didelphis virginiana

Size: 25-40 in. (64-102 cm)
Description: Grayish fur, white face, black-tipped ears and naked, rat-like tail.
Habitat: Woodlands, farming areas, forest edges, suburban areas.
Comments: Most active in the evening and at night. It has the peculiar habit of pretending to be dead (playing 'possum') when frightened. An introduced species now widespread in California.

INSECTIVORES

Insectivores are generally small mammals with long snouts, short legs and sharp teeth. They live on or under the ground and feed on insects and other invertebrates.

ORNATE SHREW
Sorex ornatus

Size: 3-4 in. (8-10 cm)
Description: Gray-brown, mouse-like mammal with a pointed nose.
Habitat: Forests, wet meadows, chaparral forests, grasslands.
Comments: Shrews are exceedingly active and dart about under leaf litter and fallen logs on tiny runways. They have a very high metabolic rate and eat up to twice their own weight in food each day. Eleven species of shrew are found in California.

CALIFORNIA MOLE
Scapanus latimanus
Size: 5-7 in. (13-18 cm)
Description: Dark brown or gray fur, short hairy tail. Front feet broader than they are long.
Habitat: Moist soils.
Comments: Rarely seen above ground, their presence can be detected by the mounds of dirt they push up when tunneling. Four mole species are found in California.

BATS

The only true flying mammals, bats have large ears, small eyes and broad wings. Primarily nocturnal, they have developed a sophisticated sonar system – echolocation – to help them hunt insects at night. As they fly, they emit a series of high frequency sounds that bounce off objects and tell them what lies in their path. During daylight, they seek refuge in caves, trees and attics. Rarely harmful, bats are valuable in helping check insect populations. Twenty-three species occur in California.

BRAZILIAN FREE-TAILED BAT
Tadarida brasiliensis
Size: 4-5 in. (10-12 cm)
Description: Small chocolate-brown bat with velvety fur and a tail extending beyond the wing membrane.
Habitat: Roosts in caves and buildings.
Comments: Typically lives in large colonies of several thousand individuals.

CALIFORNIA MYOTIS
Myotis californicus
Size: 2-3 in. (5-8 cm)
Description: Distinguished by its small size. Coat is buff to brown with the hair bases much darker-colored than the tips.
Habitat: Crevices in caves, buildings, deserts, rocky areas.
Comments: Occurs in small colonies or singly. Often hawks for insects near the lower branches of trees.

RABBITS AND ALLIES

Members of this distinctive group of mammals have long ears, large eyes and long hind legs. Primarily nocturnal, they commonly rest in protected areas like thickets during the day. When threatened, they thump their hind feet on the ground as an alarm signal. Eight species occur in California.

BRUSH RABBIT
Sylvilagus bachmani

Size: 12-15 in. (30-38 cm)
Description: Small, brownish rabbit with short ears and a small tail.
Habitat: Thick brushy areas, chaparral.
Comments: Often spotted feeding at dusk and dawn. Young are active during the day.

DESERT COTTONTAIL
Sylvilagus auduboni

Size: 14-18 in. (36-46 cm)
Description: Larger than the brush rabbit with longer hind legs, medium-sized ears and a large white tail.
Habitat: Dry grasslands, open plains and deserts.
Comments: Feeds on a range of plants including grasses, mesquite and cactus. Uses stumps and sloping trees as lookouts.

BLACK-TAILED JACKRABBIT
Lepus californicus

Size: 20-25 in. (51-64 cm)
Description: Large gray or tan rabbit with long black-tipped ears and a black-streaked tail.
Habitat: Prairies and open areas.
Comments: Very athletic, they hop up to 10 feet at a time and can reach speeds of 35 mph (56 kph). Active in late afternoon and evening.

SQUIRRELS AND ALLIES

This diverse family of hairy-tailed, large-eyed rodents includes chipmunks, tree squirrels, ground squirrels and marmots. All but the tree squirrels live in burrows on or under the ground throughout the year. Most are active during the day and easily observed in the field.

MERRIAM'S CHIPMUNK
Eutamias merriami

Size: 7-10 in. (18-25 cm)
Description: Small, gray-brown squirrel with indistinct side and face stripes.
Habitat: Mixed forests, brushland, chaparral.
Comments: Active during the day, it is very vocal and often heard twittering and chattering. Feeds mostly on seeds. The similar lodgepole chipmunk (*Eutamias speciosus*) found at higher elevations has more distinct stripes.

GRAY SQUIRREL
Sciurus griseus

Size: 17-23 in. (44-59 cm)
Description: Has a gray coat, light belly and bushy tail.
Habitat: Forested areas.
Comments: Lives in large leaf nests, usually high in trees. Active during the morning, it feeds on conifer seeds and acorns.

FLYING SQUIRREL
Glaucomys sabrinus

Size: 10-14 in. (25-36 cm)
Description: Distinguished by its gray-brown coat, whitish undersides and loose fold of skin between its front and hind legs.
Habitat: Mixed and coniferous forests.
Comments: By spreadeagling and stretching its flight skin taut, it glides between trees for distances that can exceed 150 ft. (46 m). Is the only nocturnal squirrel in the Pacific states.

CALIFORNIA GROUND SQUIRREL
Spermophilus beecheyi

Size: 14-19 in. (36-48 cm)
Description: Coat is brown to gray with white wash on neck and sides and a dark band down its back.
Habitat: Grasslands and open areas with low vegetation.
Comments: These ground-dwelling rodents are easily observed feeding in open areas and running in and out of their multi-chambered tunnels.

GOLDEN-MANTLED GROUND SQUIRREL
Spermophilus lateralis

Size: 9-12 in. (23-30 cm)
Description: Told by its coppery head and shoulders and long white side stripe bordered in black. Unlike similar-looking chipmunks, it lacks facial stripes.
Habitat: Moist coniferous forests in the mountains.
Comments: When predators approach, individuals will sound warning calls causing all to flee to the safety of their burrows. Those found near campgrounds are often very tame.

YELLOWBELLY MARMOT
Marmota flaviventris

Size: 18-28 in. (46-70 cm)
Description: Large, yellow-brown rodent with a yellow belly. Many have a white patch between the eyes.
Habitat: Rocky alpine areas to elevations of 12,000 ft. (3,650 m).
Comments: Primarily diurnal, it is conspicuous in the Sierras. Warning call is a repetitive, highly-pitched chirp.

BEAVERS

Found on rivers, lakes and marshes, beavers are the largest North American rodents. Highly aquatic, they have webbed feet and long, broad tails which they slap on the water's surface when alarmed.

BEAVER
Castor canadensis

Size: 40-47 in. (1-1.2 m)
Description: Glossy brown coat, flat, scaly tail.
Habitat: Lakes, ponds and streams.
Comments: Many beavers live in dens excavated along banks; others build cone-shaped houses of sticks and mud. Diet consists of the bark of deciduous trees and shrubs, including aspens, willows and maples.

MICE AND ALLIES

Most members of this large group have large ears, long tails and breed throughout the year. Dedicated omnivores, they have adapted to practically every North American habitat.

DEER MOUSE
Peromyscus maniculatus

Size: 4-8 in. (10-20 cm)
Description: Bicolored coat is pale gray to red-brown above and white below. Long, hairy tail is also bicolored.
Habitat: Common and widespread in a variety of habitats.
Comments: Feeds on seeds, buds, fruit and wild plants. Active year-round.

HOUSE MOUSE
Mus musculus

Size: 5-8 in. (13-20 cm)
Description: Told by its gray coat, large eyes and ears and scaly tail.
Habitat: Very common near human dwellings.
Comments: Normally lives in colonies. Females have up to 5 litters of 4-8 young annually.

CALIFORNIA VOLE
Microtus californicus

Size: 6-8 in. (15-20 cm)
Description: Brown-black mouse-sized mammal with pale feet and a short, bicolored tail.
Habitat: Forests, swamps and grassy meadows.
Comments: Eats grass, roots and seeds. Presence can be detected by the small tunnels they create under grass and snow.

NORWAY RAT
Rattus norvegicus

Size: 12-18 in. (30-45 cm)
Description: Large gray brown rodent with a scaly tail.
Habitat: Common near human dwellings.
Comments: Albino strains of this species are commonly used in lab experiments. The Black Rat (*Rattus rattus*) is also found in California.

DUSKY-FOOTED WOODRAT
Neotoma fuscipes

Size: 12-18 in. (30-45 cm)
Description: Large gray-brown rat with light underparts and a hairy tail.
Habitat: Chaparral, mixed forests, Sierra foothills.
Comments: Often builds large, cone-shaped stick houses that are conspicuous near trails.

WESTERN JUMPING MOUSE
Zapus princeps

Size: 8-10 in. (20-25 cm)
Description: Coat is olive above, yellowish on the sides and white below. Large hind legs and long tail assist it in bounding across the ground.
Habitat: Found in mountain meadows and open woodlands near water.
Comments: Capable of leaping up to 6 ft. (2 m).

PORCUPINES

Porcupines are dark mammals with coats of stiff, barbed quills. When threatened, they face away from their aggressor, erect the quills and lash out with their tail. The loosely rooted quills detach on contact and are extremely difficult to remove.

PORCUPINE
Erethizon dorsatum

Size: 25-35 in. (64-89 cm)
Description: Chunky profile, arched back and long gray coat of barbed quills.
Habitat: Common in forests and shrubby ravines.
Comments: Feeds on leaves, twigs and bark and spends much of its time in trees.

RACCOONS AND ALLIES

All members of this diverse family of dog-sized mammals have ringed tails.

RACCOON
Procyon lotor

Size: 25-40 in. (64-102 cm)
Description: Gray-brown coat, black mask and ringed tail.
Habitat: Wooded areas near water throughout California.
Comments: Feeds on small animals, insects, plants and refuse and often dunks its food into water before eating it. Primarily nocturnal.

RINGTAIL
Bassariscus astutus

Size: 24-30 in. (61-76 cm)
Description: Has large eyes, large ears and a long ringed tail. Lacks a black mask.
Habitat: Rocky areas, rough country, chaparral.
Comments: Hunts at night, killing prey with a bite to the neck. Nicknamed 'Miners' Cats,' they were once used to control rodent populations in mines.

WEASELS AND ALLIES

Members of this group usually have small heads, long necks, short legs and long bodies. All but sea otters have prominent anal scent glands which are used for social and sexual communication.

LONG-TAILED WEASEL
Mustela frenata

Size: 13-18 in. (33-46 cm)
Description: Told by slender body and long, black-tipped tail. Summer coat is brown above, white below with brown feet. Above 4,000 ft. (1,220 m) the winter coat is all white except for black tip on tail.
Habitat: Found near water in open woodlands, meadows and fields.
Comments: Weasels are aggressive hunters which are notorious for killing more prey than they can eat.

MINK
Mustela vison

Size: 20-25 in. (51-64 cm)
Description: Told by rich brown coat; often has white spotting on chin and throat.
Habitat: Common near water in a variety of habitats.
Comments: Highly aquatic, they den along river and stream banks and feed on fish, amphibians, crustaceans and small mammals.

STRIPED SKUNK
Mephitis mephitis

Size: 20-30 in. (51-76 cm)
Description: Black mammal with thin white forehead stripe and two white back stripes.
Habitat: Open wooded areas, farmland, suburbs.
Comments: Protects itself by spraying aggressors with noxious-smelling musk from its anal glands. Spray effective to 20 ft. (6 m) away. Feeds on vegetation, insects and small mammals.

SPOTTED SKUNK
Spilogale gracilis

Size: 9-14 in. (23-36 cm)
Description: Black coat has 4-6 irregular stripes. White spots on head and sides.
Habitat: Mixed woodlands, wastelands.
Comments: When threatened, it gives fair warning by raising its tail, doing a handstand and spreading its hind feet before spraying. A good climber and swimmer, it is more agile than larger skunks.

BADGER
Taxidea taxus

Size: 20-24 in. (51-61 cm)
Description: A squat, heavy-bodied animal with a long yellow-gray coat, white forehead stripe and long foreclaws.
Habitat: Grasslands and uncultivated pastures.
Comments: A prodigious burrower that feeds mostly on ground squirrels and other burrowing mammals.

SEA OTTER
Enhydra lutris

Size: 30-60 in. (75-150 cm)
Description: Long-bodied, glossy brown mammal with short legs, webbed feet and a thick tail. Face is yellowish.
Habitat: Kelp beds.
Comments: Resembles the river otter (*Lutra canadensis*) found in lakes and rivers in northern California. Feeds floating on its back and often uses a stone to break open shellfish and sea urchins.

DOGS

Members of this family have long snouts, erect ears and resemble domestic dogs in looks and habit. Active year-round.

GRAY FOX
Urocyon cinereoargenteus

Size: 30-45 in. (76-114 cm)
Description: Distinguished by its coat that is blackish-gray above and rusty-white below.
Habitat: Wooded lowlands, swamps, chaparral.
Comments: A secretive, nocturnal species, it sometimes forages during the day. An excellent climber, it often seeks refuge in trees.

COYOTE
Canis latrans

Size: 40-50 in. (1-1.3 m)
Description: Yellow-gray dog with a pointed nose, rusty legs and ears and a bushy, black-tipped tail.
Habitat: Wooded and open areas.
Comments: Largely a nocturnal hunter, it is often seen loping across fields at dawn and dusk. Holds tail down when running. Feeds on rodents, rabbits, berries and carrion.

CATS

These highly specialized carnivores are renowned hunters. All have short faces, keen vision, powerful bodies and retractable claws. Most are nocturnal hunters.

MOUNTAIN LION
Felis concolor

Size: 6-8 ft. (1.8-2.4 m)
Description: Large tan cat has a whitish belly and long, black-tipped tail.
Habitat: Forests and chaparral in the mountains and foothills.
Comments: A solitary hunter, it feeds largely on cloven-hoofed mammals, hares and other small mammals. Also called cougar and puma.

BOBCAT
Felis rufus

Size: 3-4 ft. (.9-1.2 m)
Description: Told by its spotted red-brown coat and short, black-striped tail.
Habitat: Scrubby open woodlands, thickets, marshes.
Comments: Named for its 'bobbed' tail, it rests in thickets by day and hunts rabbits and rodents by night. Has a variety of calls similar to a domestic cat.

BEARS

This group includes the largest terrestrial carnivores in the world. All are heavy-bodied, large-headed animals, with short ears and small tails. Their sense of smell is keen, though eyesight is generally poor.

BLACK BEAR
Ursus americanus

Size: 4-6 ft. (1.2-1.8 m)
Description: Coat is normally black, but cinnamon and blue-gray variants also occur.
Habitat: Primarily mountainous areas.
Comments: Diet is 85% vegetarian and consists of berries, vegetation, fish, insects, mammals and refuse. Scavenges much of the meat it eats.

HOOFED MAMMALS

This general grouping includes members of the deer and sheep families.

MULE DEER
Odocoileus hemionus

Size: 4-6 ft. (1.2-1.8 m)
Description: Distinguished by tan coat, large 'mule-sized' ears and black-tipped tail.
Habitat: Open forests and wooded river valleys, chaparral.
Comments: Essentially a solitary species, mule deer often form herds during mating season and winter. They feed mostly on shrubs, twigs and grasses. Males shed antlers January-March.

ELK
Cervus elaphus

Size: 6-9 ft. (1.8-2.7 m)
Description: Large deer with shaggy brown neck and light rump patch.
Habitat: Mountain meadows and open forests.
Comments: Subspecies of elk including tule elk and Roosevelt elk are protected on a number of reserves in California. Males shed antlers annually.

BIGHORN SHEEP
Ovis canadensis

Size: 5-6 ft. (1.5-1.8 m)
Description: Told by large coiled horns and white rump patch.
Habitat: Meadows in the mountains and foothills near rugged slopes.
Comments: Powerful climbers, they have specialized 'suction-cup' hooves which enhance their traction on rocky slopes. Males and females form separate herds for most of the year. Horns are never shed.

MARINE MAMMALS

This group includes a variety of mammals that live in the water. Sea lions and seals are carnivores that spend the majority of their time at sea, but come ashore to breed. The fish-like dolphins and whales spend all their time in the water, breathing air through blowholes set high on their heads. Unlike fish, all marine mammals have horizontal, rather than vertical, tail flukes.

CALIFORNIA SEA LION
Zalophus californicus

Size: 5-8 ft. (1.5-2.4 m)
Description: Coat is brown when dry, black when wet. Males have high foreheads and are much larger than females.
Habitat: Found along sandy and rocky shorelines in colonies.
Comments: Males are very vocal, continually honking at one another when defending their territory. Diet consists of fish and squid.

HARBOR SEAL
Phoca vitulina

Size: 4-7 ft. (1.2-2.1 m)
Description: Has a dark-spotted yellow-brown coat. Also called 'leopard seal.'
Habitat: Coastal waters, harbors, bays.
Comments: Found basking along shorelines at all times of the day, often in large groups. Much less vocal than sea lion.

NORTHERN ELEPHANT SEAL
Mirounga angustirostris

Size: To 21 ft. (6.5 m)
Description: Huge brown seals. Adult males have a large, over-hanging snout and weigh up to 8,000 lbs. (3,628 kg).
Habitat: Sandy beaches from central to southern California.
Comments: Bulls battle each other for females and breeding territories from December to March.

PACIFIC WHITE-SIDED DOLPHIN
Lagenorhynchus obliquidens

Size: 6-9 ft. (1.8-2.7 m)
Description: Told by green-black body, pale side stripes and white belly.
Habitat: Spotted near shorelines in winter and spring.
Comments: Travels in large groups of up to 1,000. Feeds primarily on small fish and squid.

COMMON DOLPHIN
Delphinus delphis

Size: 6-8 ft. (1.8-2.4 m)
Description: Distinguished by its dark flippers, yellowish flanks and white belly.
Habitat: Deep and nearshore waters.
Comments: Travels in large schools and often follows ships.

DALL'S PORPOISE
Phocoenoides dalli

Size: 5-6 ft. (1.5-1.8 m)
Description: Told by black body and large white belly patch.
Habitat: Common in coastal waters, especially in winter.
Comments: Found in groups of 2 to 20 individuals. Often plays around ships. Porpoises are generally distinguished from dolphins by their shorter snouts and stockier bodies.

KILLER WHALE
Orcinus orca
Size: 15-30 ft. (4.5-9 m)
Description: Told by jet-black body, white belly and white eye spots.
Habitat: Most abundant in coastal waters during spring and fall salmon runs.
Comments: Known as 'sea wolves,' killer whales travel in groups of up to 40 individuals.

HUMPBACK WHALE
Megaptera novaeangliae
Size: 40-50 ft. (12-15 m)
Description: Baleen whale with a humped back, and scalloped flippers and flukes.
Habitat: Coastal during migration.
Comments: The most vocal of whales, its haunting calls can be heard on the surface during calm days.

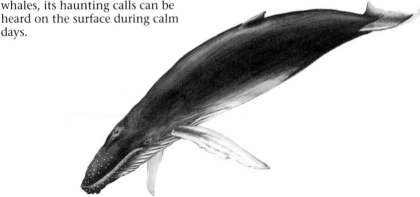

GRAY WHALE
Eschrichtius robustus

Size: To 46 ft. (14 m)
Description: Large, mottled gray-blue whale has a small dorsal hump and 2-5 throat grooves. Skin is often blotched with white barnacles.
Habitat: Abundant in coastal waters during winter-spring migration.
Comments: Breeds in waters off Baja California. California's state marine mammal.

FINBACK WHALE
Balaenoptera physalus

Size: 60-80 ft. (18-24.5 m)
Description: Large, flat-headed gray whale with light belly, and posterior dorsal fin. Back has a prominent ridge between the dorsal fin and tail.
Habitat: Found inshore and offshore throughout the year.
Comments: A baleen whale, it has a sieve-like structure in its mouth that is used to strain small crustaceans, fish and plankton from the water.

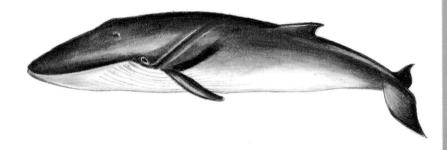

WHAT ARE BIRDS?

Birds are warm-blooded, feathered animals with two wings and two legs. The majority can fly and those that cannot are believed to be descended from ancestors that did. Adaptations for flight include hollow bones and an enhanced breathing capacity. Birds also have an efficient four-chambered heart and are insulated against the weather to enhance temperature regulation.

HOW TO IDENTIFY BIRDS

As with other species, the best way to become good at identifying birds is simply to practice. The more birds you attempt to identify, the better you'll become at distinguishing species.

When you are birding, the first thing to note is the habitat you are exploring in order to know what kinds of birds to expect. When you spot a bird, check for obvious field marks. Is it small (sparrow), medium (crow), or large (heron)? Note the shape of its beak. Look at the color and pattern of its feathers for any distinguishing markings. Does it have any unusual behavioral characteristics?

If you are interested in enhancing your field skills, it is essential to become familiar with bird songs since many species are easily distinguished by their call. Bird song tapes and CDs are available from nature stores and libraries.

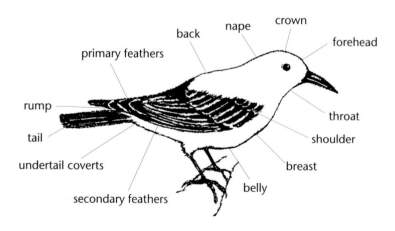

N.B. – *It is important to note that many illustrations feature the adult male in its breeding coloration. Colors and markings shown may be duller or absent during different times of the year.*

GREBES

The members of this group of duck-like birds have short tails, slender necks and stiff bills. Excellent divers, they have lobed toes rather than webbed feet and have legs located near the back of the body to help propel them through the water.

PIED-BILLED GREBE
Podilymbus podiceps

Size: 12-15 in. (30-38 cm)
Description: Distinguished by its small size and chicken-like white bill. Breeding birds have a black-banded bill and black throat. Non-breeding adults are grayish.
Habitat: Freshwater ponds, lakes and weed-choked marshes.
Comments: Often swims with body partially submerged. Hatchlings are often carried and fed on the backs of their parents

winter

summer

WESTERN GREBE
Aechmophorus occidentalis

Size: 20-30 in. (50-76 cm)
Description: Long-necked, slender-billed bird is black above, white below.
Habitat: Large lakes and coastal waters.
Comments: Winters along the coast in large numbers. Noted for their spectacular courtship display in which males and females run across the water's surface in pairs.

PELICANS AND ALLIES

These aquatic birds often perch by boats and piers along the coast.

BROWN PELICAN
Pelecanus occidentalis

Size: 3-5 ft. (1-1.5 m)
Description: Stout brownish bird with long, pouched beak, light-colored head and webbed feet.
Habitat: Coastal.
Comments: Slow flier that skims along the water's surface. Catches fish by plunging into the ocean. The white pelican (*Pelacanus erythrohynchos*) is found on inland lakes.

DOUBLE-CRESTED CORMORANT
Phalacrocorax auritus

Size: 30-36 in. (76-90 cm)
Description: Black bird distinguished by its slender neck, hooked bill and orange throat patch. Often perches with wings spread to allow them to dry. Head crests are rarely evident.
Habitat: Common in coastal waters, some found inland.
Comments: Nest in colonies on rocky ledges. Swims with bill pointed upward at an angle.

HERONS AND ALLIES

Large wading birds with long legs, long necks and slender bills. Most inhabit marshes and other shallows where they feed on fish, frogs and insects. Sexes are similar. All fly with their necks folded into an 'S' curve.

GREAT BLUE HERON
Ardea herodias

Size: 40-52 in. (1-1.3 m)
Description: Large, slender bluish bird with long legs, a long, yellowish bill and white face. Black plumes extend back from the eye.
Habitat: Wetlands, margins of ponds, lakes and watercourses.
Comments: Often seen stalking fish and frogs in still waters.

SNOWY EGRET
Egretta thula

Size: 20-26 in. (51-66 cm)
Description: Slender white bird with a black bill, black legs and yellow feet. Feathery back and neck plumes are present during breeding season.
Habitat: Marshes, ponds, tidal flats.
Comments: Is slowly recovering from near extinction earlier this century.

AMERICAN BITTERN
Botaurus lentiginosus

Size: 20-30 in. (51-76 cm)
Description: Brown bird with a thick, streaked neck and black whisker mark.
Habitat: Marshes.
Comments: Common but elusive, it can be easily identified by its call that sounds like a rusty water pump – *oonck-er-lunk*. Often hides among reeds by freezing in position with its bill pointed upwards.

GEESE

Geese are large, long-necked birds found near ponds and marshes. Highly terrestrial, they are often spotted grazing in fields and meadows. Their diet consists largely of grasses, grains and some aquatic plants. Noisy in flight, they are often heard before they're seen passing overhead.

CANADA GOOSE
Branta canadensis

Size: 24-40 in. (60-100 cm)
Description: Told by black head and neck, and white cheek patch.
Habitat: Near marshes, ponds, lakes and rivers.
Comments: Geese fly in a 'V' formation when migrating. Pairs usually mate for life. Call is a nasal *honk*.

SNOW GOOSE
Chen caerulescens

Size: 25-30 in. (64-76 cm)
Description: White goose with an orange bill, orange feet and black wing tips.
Habitat: Marshes, sloughs, shallow lakes.
Comments: Very common in central California during winter months.

DUCKS AND ALLIES

Smaller than geese, ducks have shorter necks and are primarily aquatic. In most, breeding males are more brightly colored than females. Both sexes have a brightly-colored band (speculum) on the trailing edge of the wing.

MALLARD
Anas platyrhynchos

Size: 20-28 in. (52-71 cm)
Description: Male has green head, white collar and chestnut breast. Female is mottled brown. Both have a metallic blue speculum.
Habitat: Ponds and marshes.
Comments: The ancestor of domestic ducks. Call is a loud *quack*.

NORTHERN PINTAIL
Anas acuta

Size: 20-30 in. (47-76 cm)
Description: Distinguished by its long neck and pointed tail. Male has a white breast and a white neck stripe. Both sexes have a glossy brown speculum which is bordered in white.
Habitat: Shallow marshes and ponds.
Comments: The most widely distributed duck in North America.

GREEN-WINGED TEAL
Anas crecca

Size: 12-15 in. (30-38 cm)
Description: Male has chestnut head and a green eye patch. Female is brown-gray with a green speculum.
Habitat: Lakes and ponds.
Comments: Fast fliers that travel in tight flocks.

CINNAMON TEAL
Anas cyanoptera
Size: 14-17 in. (36-43 cm)
Description: Both sexes have a chalky blue forewing patch. Males are bright cinnamon; females are mottled brown.
Habitat: Marshes, shallow ponds and rivers.
Comments: The forewing patches are most visible in flight.

AMERICAN WIGEON
Anas americana
Size: 18-23 in. (46-58 cm)
Description: Male is brownish with a gray head and a glossy green face patch. Female has a bluish bill and flecked head. Speculum is green.
Habitat: Freshwater streams, lakes, marshes.
Comments: Though primarily aquatic, these ducks can often be found nibbling grass on the shores of ponds and marshes.

NORTHERN SHOVELER
Anas clypeata
Size: 17-20 in. (43-50 cm)
Description: Told by its flat head and large, spatulate bill. Male has a green head, rusty sides and a blue wing patch.
Habitat: Fresh- and saltwater marshes, lakes, ponds.
Comments: Shovel-shaped bill is used to strain aquatic animals and vegetation from the water. Swims with bill pointed downward.

WHITE-WINGED SCOTER
Melanitta fusca

Size: 19-23 in. (48-58 cm)
Description: Told by dark plumage and light face patches. Male has a swollen bill.
Habitat: Coastal, deep freshwater lakes and large rivers.
Comments: Often found in large flocks.

COMMON MERGANSER
Mergus merganser

Size: 22-27 in. (56-69 cm)
Description: Told by sleek profile and long, slender bill. Male has an iridescent black-green head and white underparts. Female has a crested rufous head and a sharply defined white throat.
Habitat: Wooded lakes and rivers.
Comments: A diving duck, it feeds primarily on fish.

COOTS

Coots are chicken-billed birds often found in the company of ducks and geese. They are, however, more closely related to cranes than ducks.

AMERICAN COOT
Fulica americana

Size: 13-16 in. (33-41 cm)
Description: Dark bird with a chicken-like white bill, white rear, long greenish legs and lobed toes.
Habitat: Freshwater in the summer and fresh- and saltwater in winter.
Comments: Feeds on the shore and in the water. Habitually pumps its head back and forth when swimming.

HAWKS, EAGLES AND ALLIES

Primarily carnivorous, these birds have sharp talons for grasping prey and sharply hooked bills for tearing into flesh. Many soar on wind currents when hunting. Sexes are similar in most.

CALIFORNIA CONDOR
Gymnogyps californianus

Size: 40-55 in. (1-1.4 m)
Description: Huge black bird with a naked head and hooked bill. White triangles on the underside of the wings are visible in flight.
Habitat: Mountains and open country.
Comments: An endangered species, it is the largest bird of prey in North America. Once nearly extinct, hand-raised populations have made a comeback in recent years and are slowly being transplanted in the wild

TURKEY VULTURE
Cathartes aura

Size: 26-32 in. (66-81 cm)
Description: Large, brown-black bird with a naked red head.
Habitat: Dry, open country.
Comments: Feeds on carrion and is often seen along roadsides. Also called a buzzard.

GOLDEN EAGLE
Aquila chrysaetos

Size: 30-40 in. (76-102 cm)
Description: Large, dark soaring bird with long, broad wings. Size distinguishes it from smaller hawks.
Habitat: Mountain regions.
Comments: Feeds on mammals, some birds and carrion. Often builds nests on power poles.

BALD EAGLE
Haliaeetus leucocephalus

Size: 30-40 in. (76-102 cm)
Description: Large dark bird with a white head and tail, and yellow legs and bill.
Habitat: Near water. Most common in northern California.
Comments: Feeds on fish and water birds. An endangered species, its local populations are well on the road to recovery.

OSPREY
Pandion haliaetus

Size: 20-25 in. (51-64 cm)
Description: Large hawk with dark brown back, light underparts and a dark eye stripe.
Habitat: Coastal, inland lakes and rivers.
Comments: Unlike most soaring birds, it glides with its wings arched. Often hovers over the water before diving after fish.

RED-TAILED HAWK
Buteo jamaicensis

Size: 20-25 in. (51-64 cm)
Description: Dark, broad-winged, wide-tailed hawk with light underparts and a red tail.
Habitat: Open fields and forests, farmlands.
Comments: This familiar hawk is often spotted perched on roadside telephone poles and fence posts.

AMERICAN KESTREL
Falco sparverius

Size: 10-12 in. (25-30 cm)
Description: Small falcon with a rusty back and tail, and pointed, narrow, spotted blue wings. Males have black facial marks
Habitat: Wooded and open areas.
Comments: Formerly called the 'sparrow hawk.' Often pumps tail when perching.

CHICKEN-LIKE BIRDS

Ground-dwelling birds that are chicken-like in looks and habit. Most have stout bills, rounded wings and heavy bodies. Primarily terrestrial, they are capable of short bursts of flight.

CALIFORNIA QUAIL
Lophortyx californicus

Size: 9-11 in. (23-28 cm)
Description: Plump bird with blue chest, black face and forward-curving plume (teardrop topknot).
Habitat: Mixed woodlands, open brushy areas, suburban parks.
Comments: Flocks descend on city parks and gardens after breeding season to feed on seeds and invertebrates. California's state bird.

RING-NECKED PHEASANT
Phasianus colchicus

Size: 30-36 in. (76-91 cm)
Description: Told at a glance by its large size, long tail, green head and white neck ring. Female is mottled brown with a long tail.
Habitat: Brushy areas, farmland, woodland edges.
Comments: Widely introduced in the Central Valley.

PLOVERS

These wading birds are distinguished from sandpipers by their thick necks, short bills and large eyes. Active feeders, they characteristically move about in quick, short sprints. Sexes are similar.

KILLDEER
Charadrius vociferus

Size: 8-11 in. (20-28 cm)
Description: Brown bird with a white breast and two black neck bands. Rump shows orange in flight. Shrill call – *kill-dee* – is repeated continuously.
Habitat: Fields, pastures, parks, open areas.
Comments: Adults often feign injury to lure intruders away from their nesting area.

SHOREBIRDS

This group of wading birds are normally found along shorelines. Most have slender bills which they use to probe in sand and mud for invertebrates. Sexes are similar in most.

LEAST SANDPIPER
Calidris minutilla

Size: 5-7 in. (13-18 cm)
Description: A small brownish bird with a short, thin bill and yellowish legs.
Habitat: Mudflats, bogs, shorelines, wet fields.
Comments: A very common shorebird, it is relatively tame and can be closely approached. Call is a *peep*.

SANDERLING
Calidris alba

Size: 7-8 in. (18-20 cm)
Description: Plump, white-bellied shorebird with a black bill and legs. Upper plumage is rusty in summer, gray in winter.
Habitat: Common on sandy shorelines and tidal flats.
Comments: Easily spotted on ocean shorelines running in and out with the waves. Feeds on tiny creatures that are 'beached' as the waves recede.

SPOTTED SANDPIPER
Actitis macularia

Size: 6-8 in. (15-20 cm)
Description: Small brown bird with light, dark-spotted underparts and spindly, yellowish legs. Spots are evident during breeding season.
Habitat: Near water with vegetated shorelines.
Comments: A solitary bird, it teeters back and forth when walking. Flies with quivering wings held downward, alternating with low glides.

COMMON SNIPE
Gallinago gallinago

Size: 10-12 in. (25-30 cm)
Description: Stocky, long-billed shorebird with a spotted breast and streaked back.
Habitat: Marshes, ponds, bogs, wet fields.
Comments: When flushed it gives a sharp cry and flies off erratically.

LONG-BILLED CURLEW
Numenius americanus

Size: 20-26 in. (50-66 cm)
Description: Distinguished by its large size, buff-brown plumage and long, downcurved bill.
Habitat: Open areas near water.
Comments: Shows bright cinnamon wing linings in flight. Voice is a loud *cur-lew!, cur-lew!*

AMERICAN AVOCET
Recurvirostra americana
Size: 15-20 in. (38-51 cm)
Description: Large shorebird with long legs and a long upcurved bill. Breeding birds have a tawny head and neck.
Habitat: Shallow ponds, marshes, mudflats.
Comments: Feeds by working bill side to side while walking through the water.

BLACK-NECKED STILT
Himantopus mexicanus
Size: 12-15 in. (30-38 cm)
Description: Very long-legged, black and white wader with a thin bill.
Habitat: Sea and lake shores, mudflats.
Comments: Common in fresh- and saltwater habitats.

BLACK OYSTERCATCHER
Haematopus bachmani
Size: 15-20 in. (38-51 cm)
Description: Black shorebird with a red bill.
Habitat: Rocky sea shores.
Comments: The stout bill is used to pry or break open shellfish. Call is a piercing whistle.

GULLS

These long-winged, web-footed birds are strong fliers and excellent swimmers. Adults are typically gray and white; immature birds are brownish. Most have square tails and are distinguished from each other by wing patterns and bill color. Eighteen species occur in California.

CALIFORNIA GULL
Larus californicus

Size: 20-23 in. (51-58 cm)
Description: Told by its gray back, white-spotted, black wing tips and greenish legs.
Habitat: Inland lakes and ponds during breeding season, coastal shorelines in winter.
Comments: The similar herring gull (*Larus argentatus*) found along the coast is distinguished by its pinkish legs.

WESTERN GULL
Larus occidentalis

Size: 24-27 in. (61-69 cm)
Description: Dark-backed gull with snowy-white underparts and pinkish legs.
Habitat: Coastal, rarely inland.
Comments: Varied diet includes carrion, garbage, eggs, young birds and aquatic animals.

DOVES

These familiar birds are common and widespread. All species coo. They feed largely on seeds, grain and insects.

ROCK DOVE
Columba livia

Size: 12-14 in. (30-36 cm)
Description: Blue-gray bird with a white rump and black-banded tail. White, tan and brown variants also exist.
Habitat: Common in cities, towns and farmlands.
Comments: This introduced species is relatively tame and can be trained for homing.

MOURNING DOVE
Zenaida macroura

Size: 11-13 in. (28-33 cm)
Description: Slender tawny bird with a long, pointed tail.
Habitat: Open woodlands, suburbs, farmlands.
Comments: Named for its mournful, cooing song. Feeds on the ground.

CUCKOOS AND ALLIES

Members have long tails and curved bills. Sexes are similar.

ROADRUNNER
Geococcyx californianus

Size: 20-24 in. (51-61 cm)
Description: Long-legged, gray-brown bird with a crested head and long tail.
Habitat: Deserts, chaparral, open country.
Comments: A ground-dwelling bird, it will fly only if forced. Feeds on small mammals, snakes and insects.

OWLS

These square-shaped birds of prey have large heads, large eyes and hooked bills. Large flattened areas around each eye help to amplify sound toward external ear flaps. Sexes are similar.

GREAT HORNED OWL
Bubo virginianus

Size: 20-25 in. (51-64 cm)
Description: Dark brown with heavily barred plumage, ear tufts, yellow eyes and white throat.
Habitat: Forests and woodlands.
Comments: Primarily nocturnal, it feeds on small mammals and birds. Sometimes spotted hunting during the day. Voice is a deep, resonant *hoo-hoo-hooooo*.

GOATSUCKERS

These nocturnal insect-eaters have large, swallow-like heads. Ancients believed that the birds used their huge gaping mouths to suck the milk of goats.

COMMON NIGHTHAWK
Chordeiles minor

Size: 8-10 in. (20-25 cm)
Description: Told by large head, short bill, white wing bars and white throat. Long, pointed wings extend beyond the tail when perching.
Habitat: Forests, open country, cities.
Comments: Spectacular fliers, they can often be seen hawking for insects during daylight.

HUMMINGBIRDS

The smallest birds, hummingbirds are named for the noise made by their wings during flight. All have long needle-like bills and extensible tongues which are used to extract nectar from flowers.

ANNA'S HUMMINGBIRD
Calypte anna

Size: 3-4 in. (8-10 cm)
Description: Small, metallic-green bird. Male has red throat and forehead. Female has spotted throat.
Habitat: Chaparral, gardens, open woods.
Comments: When defending their territory, males will often swoop down to 'buzz' intruders.

KINGFISHERS

Solitary, broad-billed birds renowned for their fishing expertise.

BELTED KINGFISHER
Megaceryle alcyon

Size: 10-14 in. (25-36 cm)
Description: Stocky, crested blue-gray bird with a large head and bill.
Habitat: Near wooded ponds, lakes and rivers.
Comments: Often seen perched over clear water. Hovers over water before plunging in headfirst after fish.

WOODPECKERS

These strong-billed birds are usually spotted on tree trunks chipping away bark in search of insects. All have stiff tails which act like props as they forage. In spring, males drum on dead limbs and other resonant objects (e.g. garbage cans, drainpipes) to establish their territories. Seventeen species occur in California.

DOWNY WOODPECKER
Picoides pubescens

Size: 5-7 in. (13-18 cm)
Description: A small, sparrow-sized, black-and-white woodpecker with a small bill. Males have a red head patch.
Habitat: Wooded areas.
Comments: Occurs in the same habitat as the similar, larger, hairy woodpecker (*Picoides villosus*).

NORTHERN FLICKER
Colaptes auratus

Size: 10-13 in. (25-33 cm)
Description: Brownish woodpecker with a spotted breast and black bib. 'Yellow-shafted' morphs have a red nape patch and yellow wing linings; males have a black 'mustache.' 'Red-shafted' morphs have reddish wing linings; males have a red 'mustache.'
Habitat: Rural and urban woodlands, desert.
Comments: White rump patch is conspicuous in flight.

ACORN WOODPECKER
Melanerpes formicivorus

Size: 8-10 in. (20-25 cm)
Description: A dark woodpecker with a yellowish face, red crown and a dark goatee.
Habitat: Oak and pine forests.
Comments: Feeds on acorns and nuts. During fall harvest, it crams these into tight holes to prevent theft by squirrels.

FLYCATCHERS

These compact birds characteristically sit on exposed perches and dart out to capture passing insects. Twenty-seven species occur here.

ASH-THROATED FLYCATCHER
Myiarchus cinerascens

Size: 7-8 in. (18-20 cm)
Description: Is olive above, yellow below with a white throat and a rusty tail.
Habitat: Woodlands, deserts.
Comments: Often nests in cavities of rotting trees.

LARKS

Terrestrial, slender-billed birds found in fields with low vegetation.

HORNED LARK
Eremophila alpestris

Size: 7-8 in. (18-20 cm)
Description: Brown bird with a yellow face, dark neck and eye marks and black 'horns.'
Habitat: Open areas including fields, shorelines, farmlands and parks.
Comments: Nests and feeds on the ground. Often found in flocks.

SWALLOWS

These acrobatic fliers have short bills, long pointed wings and long tails (often forked). Their wide mouths are adapted for scooping up insects on the wing. Seven species occur in California.

VIOLET-GREEN SWALLOW
Tachycineta thalassina

Size: 4-6 in. (10-15 cm)
Description: Plumage is glossy green-purple above, white below. White flank patches nearly meet above the tail.
Habitat: Open and semi-wooded areas in towns, farms and foothills.
Comments: Often seen perched in groups along power lines and fences. Flight is undulating and graceful.

CROWS AND ALLIES

These large, omnivorous birds are very common. Sexes are similar.

STELLER'S JAY
Cyanocitta stelleri

Size: 12-14 in. (30-36 cm)
Description: Distinguished by its sooty plumage and prominent blue-gray head crest.
Habitat: Coniferous and pine-oak forests.
Comments: Very gregarious, it often frequents campsites and human dwellings in search of handouts.

SCRUB JAY
Aphelocoma californicus

Size: 11-13 in. (28-33 cm)
Description: A streamlined blue bird with a long bill and tail. Key field marks are white throat, incomplete blue necklace and brown back.
Habitat: Oak-chaparral, woodlands.
Comments: Common in cities and towns. Flight is undulating and short, followed by a sweeping glide.

CLARK'S NUTCRACKER
Nucifraga columbiana

Size: 12-13 in. (30-33 cm)
Description: Light gray bird with a white face, long, sharply-pointed bill and long tail.
Habitat: Coniferous forests near the timberline.
Comments: Common near alpine campsites throughout the year, it occasionally wanders to low country in winter.

COMMON CROW
Corvus brachyrhynchos

Size: 18-22 in. (46-56 cm)
Description: Black bird with a thick black bill. Call is a distinct *caw*.
Habitat: Fields, beaches, forests, parks, cities.
Comments: Abundant and widespread, they do a valuable service in controlling insect populations.

COMMON RAVEN
Corvus corax

Size: 22-27 in. (56-69 cm)
Description: Similar to the crow, it is distinguished by its larger size, heavier beak, wedge-shaped tail and low, croaking call.
Habitat: Wilderness and open country.
Comments: An opportunistic feeder, it feeds on carrion and is often seen near garbage dumps.

NUTHATCHES

Nuthatches are stout little birds with thin, sharp bills and stumpy tails. They are usually spotted clambering about on tree trunks and branches.

WHITE-BREASTED NUTHATCH
Sitta carolinensis

Size: 5-6 in. (13-15 cm)
Description: Chunky, white-faced, grayish bird with black cap, white underparts and short, sharp bill.
Habitat: Coniferous and mixed wood forests.
Comments: Habitually creeps about on tree trunks and branches searching for insects, often descending head first.

WRENS

These little brown birds have the distinctive habit of cocking their tails in the air. They spend much of their time on the ground foraging for insects on leaves and branches. Eight species occur in California.

HOUSE WREN
Troglodytes aedon

Size: 4-5 in. (10-13 cm)
Description: Distinguished by its barred tail, slender bill and cocked tail.
Habitat: Thickets, wooded areas, farmlands, towns.
Comments: An aggressive little bird, it moves about in quick, jerky motions, often scolding intruders. Common at birdbaths and feeders.

MOCKINGBIRDS AND THRASHERS

Long-tailed birds with slender, decurved bills, they often sing loudly from exposed perches.

CALIFORNIA THRASHER
Toxostoma redivivum

Size: 10-13 in. (25-33 cm)
Description: Robin-sized gray-brown bird with long, downturned bill.
Habitat: Chaparral, parks, gardens.
Comments: Spends much of its time on the ground searching for insects and invertebrates.

MOCKINGBIRD
Mimus polyglottos

Size: 9-11 in. (23-28 cm)
Description: Robin-sized, gray-brown bird with a downturned bill and a long tail.
Habitat: Chaparral, scrubby woodlands, gardens.
Comments: Named for its habit of mimicking distinctive sounds like the calls of other birds.

THRUSHES

This group of woodland birds includes many good singers. Sexes are similar in most.

AMERICAN ROBIN
Turdus migratorius

Size: 9-11 in. (23-28 cm)
Description: Familiar to most, it is told by its gray back and rusty breast.
Habitat: Very common in towns, fields and open woodlands.
Comments: Forages on the ground for insects, snails and worms.

WESTERN BLUEBIRD
Sialia mexicana

Size: 9-10 in. (23-25 cm)
Description: Male is bright blue above with a rusty breast and white belly. Female is brownish with dull blue wings and tail.
Habitat: Open woods, farmlands.
Comments: Often sits on conspicuous perches when hunting for insects.

WAXWINGS

These gregarious birds are named for their red wing marks which look like waxy droplets.

CEDAR WAXWING
Bombycilla cedrorum

Size: 6-8 in. (15-20 cm)
Description: Told at a glance by its sleek, crested head, yellow belly, yellow-tipped tail and red wing marks.
Habitat: Open deciduous woods, orchards, suburbs.
Comments: Diet consists largely of berries and insects. Occurs in small flocks.

SILKY FLYCATCHERS

This tropical bird is found in hot, open areas with tall trees.

PHAINOPEPLA
Phainopepla nitens

Size: 7-8 in. (18-20 cm)
Description: Glossy blue-black male has crested head and white wing patches (conspicuous in flight). Grayish female has slender crest. Both sexes have red eyes.
Habitat: Oak woodlands, chaparral, mesquite, desert scrub.
Comments: Feeds on mistletoe berries and insects.

STARLINGS

These fat-bodied, short-tailed birds are abundant in cities and towns.

EUROPEAN STARLING
Sturnus vulgaris

Size: 6-8 in. (15-20 cm)
Description: Chubby bird with iridescent black-purple plumage and a pointed yellow bill.
Habitat: Farms, fields, cities, deserts.
Comments: Considered a pest by many, the starling is an aggressive bird that competes with native species for food and nesting sights. Usually travels in huge flocks.

WARBLERS AND ALLIES

Members of this large family are distinguished from other small birds by their thin, pointed bills. Males tend to be more brightly-colored than females and are the only singers. Over 45 species occur in California.

YELLOW WARBLER
Dendroica petechia

Size: 4-5 in. (10-13 cm)
Description: Distinctive yellow bird with a streaked breast.
Habitat: Shrubs and thickets in river valleys, orchards and urban areas.
Comments: Song is a cheery *sweet, sweet, sweet.*

YELLOW-RUMPED WARBLER
Dendroica coronata

Size: 5-6 in. (13-15 cm)
Description: Blue-gray bird with yellow rump, cap and wing patches; throat is either white or yellow. Brownish females have markings similar to males on their throats and rumps.
Habitat: Coniferous and mixed forests.
Comments: A relatively newly designated species, formerly the myrtle and Audubon's warblers.

ORANGE-CROWNED WARBLER
Vermivora celata

Size: 4-5 in. (10-13 cm)
Description: Drab olive bird with yellowish underparts and an orange crown patch.
Habitat: Open woodland, brushy areas.
Comments: Very common. Crown patch is often concealed.

BLACKBIRDS AND ALLIES

A diverse group of birds ranging from iridescent black birds to brightly-colored meadowlarks and orioles. All have conical, sharply-pointed bills.

BROWN-HEADED COWBIRD
Molothrus ater

Size: 6-8 in. (15-20 cm)
Description: Blue-black bird with brown hood and finch-like bill.
Habitat: Open woods, farmlands and fields, often near domestic livestock.
Comments: Female is noted for her parasitic habit of laying eggs in the nests of other birds. While some species remove the new egg, most will raise the orphaned cowbird as their own, often at the expense of their own progeny.

RED-WINGED BLACKBIRD
Agelaius phoeniceus

Size: 7-9 in. (18-23 cm)
Description: Black male has distinctive red shoulder patches. Brown females look like large sparrows.
Habitat: Sloughs, marshes and wet fields.
Comments: Usually nests in reeds or tall grass near water. Normally found in large flocks.

NORTHERN ORIOLE
Icterus galbula

Size: 6-8 in. (15-20 cm)
Description: Distinctive black and orange bird. Has either a full black hood or a black cap, chin and eye stripe.
Habitat: Open deciduous forests, ranchlands.
Comments: A relatively newly designated species, formerly the Baltimore and Bullock orioles. Both build distinctive pouch-like, woven nests.

WESTERN MEADOWLARK
Sturnella neglecta

Size: 8-12 in. (20-30 cm)
Description: Mottled brown bird is distinguished by its bright yellow breast, white-edged tail, and dark V-shaped neckband.
Habitat: Grassy fields, meadows, marshes.
Comments: Loud, flute-like, gurgling song is distinctive.

TANAGERS

These brightly-colored birds of tropical orgin have heavy, conical, seed-cracking bills.

WESTERN TANAGER
Piranga ludoviciana

Size: 7 in. (18 cm)
Description: Yellow bird with a red head and dark back. Females and young are olive-colored with two light wing bars.
Habitat: Open coniferous and mixed forests.
Comments: Common near wooded picnic areas. Call is a dry *pit-ick, pit-ick.*

FINCHES, SPARROWS AND ALLIES

Members of this family are brightly-colored and have short, thick, seed-cracking bills.

AMERICAN GOLDFINCH
Carduelis tristis

Size: 4-5 in. (10-13 cm)
Description: Male is bright yellow with a black cap, black tail and wings and a white rump. Duller female lacks a cap.
Habitat: Wooded groves, gardens.
Comments: Often found in flocks. Can be identified on the wing by its deeply undulating flight. Canary-like song is bright and cheery.

HOUSE FINCH
Carpodacus mexicanus

Size: 5-6 in. (13-15 cm)
Description: Brown bird with a reddish forehead, breast and rump.
Habitat: Cities, towns, open country, bottomlands.
Comments: Highly social birds, they are easily attracted to feeders and nesting sites.

PINE SISKIN
Carduelis pinus

Size: 4-5 in. (10-13 cm)
Description: Brown bird with heavily streaked plumage and a notched tail. Small yellow patches on wings and tail are most prominent in flight.
Habitat: Coniferous and mixed forests.
Comments: Quite tame and easily attracted to feeders. Often found flocking in the tops of trees.

SONG SPARROW
Melospiza melodia

Size: 5-7 in. (13-18 cm)
Description: Distinguished by heavily-streaked breast with streaks converging to a central spot. Tail is rounded.
Habitat: Very common in bushes and woodlands near water.
Comments: Often visits feeders and birdbaths. Forages along the ground. Melodious song usually begins with 3-4 similar notes.

CHIPPING SPARROW
Spizella passerina

Size: 5-6 in. (13-15 cm)
Description: Told by red cap, white eyebrow line, unstreaked breast and notched tail.
Habitat: Open forests, fields, lawns, gardens.
Comments: Nests are often victimized by Brown-headed Cowbird. Song is a repetitive, sharp *chip*.

RUFOUS-SIDED TOWHEE
Piplio erythrophthalmus

Size: 7-9 in. (18-23 cm)
Description: Told by black hood, rufous sides, white belly and red eyes. Female is brown where male is black.
Habitat: Woodlands, wood margins, cities, usually in undergrowth.
Comments: Its dull-brown cousin, the brown towhee (*Piplib fuscus*), is also common in woods and gardens.

DARK-EYED JUNCO
Junco hyemalis

Size: 5-7 in. (13-18 cm)
Description: Key field marks are dark head, whitish bill, white belly and white-edged tail. Has gray sides and a gray back or a black head and a brown back.
Habitat: Coniferous and mixed woods, gardens, parks.
Comments: Gregarious and easily attracted to feeders. A relatively newly designated species, formerly the slate-colored junco, Oregon junco, gray-headed Junco and white-winged junco. Of these, only the first two occur in California.

WEAVER FINCHES

These sparrow-like birds were introduced to North America in 1850, and are now widespread throughout the continent.

HOUSE SPARROW
Passer domesticus

Size: 5-6 in. (13-15 cm)
Description: Black throat and brown nape of male are key field marks. Females and young are dull brown with a light eye stripe.
Habitat: Suburbs, cities, farmlands.
Comments: These gregarious, social birds gather in large flocks between breeding seasons.

WHAT ARE REPTILES AND AMPHIBIANS?

Reptiles and amphibians represent a diverse array of water- and land-dwelling animals.

REPTILES

Reptiles can generally be described as terrestrial, scaly creatures that breathe through lungs. The majority reproduce by laying eggs on land; in some, the eggs develop inside the mother who later gives birth to live young. Contrary to popular belief, very few are harmful to man; all are valuable in controlling rodent and insect populations.

The most common types of California reptiles are turtles, lizards and snakes.

AMPHIBIANS

Amphibians are smooth-skinned, limbed vertebrates that live in moist habitats and breathe through lungs, skin, gills, or a combination of all three. While they spend much of their lives on land, they still depend on a watery environment to complete their life cycle. Most reproduce by laying eggs in or near water. The young hatch as swimming larvae – tadpoles, for example – which breathe through gills. After a short developmental period, the larvae metamorphose into young adults with lungs and legs.

The most common types of California amphibians are salamanders, frogs and toads.

HOW TO IDENTIFY REPTILES AND AMPHIBIANS

Reptiles are secretive but can be observed if you know where to look. Turtles are found on the edges of ponds and lakes and often sun themselves on rocks and logs. Lizards sun themselves in habitats ranging from open deserts to suburban back yards and are easily the most conspicuous reptiles. The best time to look for snakes is in the early morning or late afternoon when it's not too hot. Look in meadows, fields, woods, or on the margins of ponds, checking under sun-warmed logs and rocks where they may be resting.

Of the amphibians, the frogs and toads are probably the easiest to observe since they loudly announce their presence during breeding season. Frogs are found in wet areas on or near the water. Toads are more terrestrial and may be found far from water, especially during the day. Salamanders are more secretive and rarely venture out of their cool, moist habitats.

TURTLES

Turtles are easily distinguished by their large bony shells, which serve to protect them from most predators. Like all reptiles, turtles breathe air through lungs; they are also able to breathe underwater from gill-like respiratory surfaces on the mouth and anus. Turtles are most active in spring during mating season. Most are omnivores and eat a wide variety of plant and animal matter.

DESERT TORTOISE
Gopherus agassizi

Size: 10-14 in. (25-36 cm)
Description: Distinguished by its brown, dome-shaped shell and thick, stumpy legs.
Habitat: Dry, sandy areas in southeast California.
Comments: A protected species, it is California's state reptile. Typically feeds at dawn and dusk and lies in a shallow burrow throughout the day.

WESTERN POND TURTLE
Clemmys marmorata

Size: 4-7 in. (10-18 cm)
Description: Told by its dark, streamlined shells. Inconspicuous lines or flecks radiate from the center of each shell segment.
Habitat: Ponds, quiet streams, marshes, ditches.
Comments: Often basks in the sun on partially submerged rocks or logs. Feeds on vegetation, crustaceans and insects.

RED-EARED SLIDER
Chrysemys scripta

Size: 5-10 in. (13-25 cm)
Description: Distinguished by its round, yellow-marked shell and wide red 'ear' stripes.
Habitat: Ponds, quiet streams, marshes, ditches.
Comments: The common pet store turtle. Many have been introduced to the wild by their owners and may outnumber native turtles in some areas.

LIZARDS

Lizards are scaly-skinned animals which usually have four legs and a tail, movable eyelids, visible ear openings, claws and toothed jaws. A few species are legless and superficially resemble snakes. They represent the largest group of living reptiles and range in size from tiny skinks to the giant 10 foot-long monitor lizards of Indonesia. Over 3,000 species are found worldwide, 95 of which occur in the U.S.

Most lizards lay eggs on or in the ground. The incubation period depends largely on the ambient temperature and the hatchlings are independent from birth. In a few species, the female retains the eggs until the young are ready to hatch.

CALIFORNIA WHIPTAIL
Cnemidophorus tigris mundus

Size: To 12 in. (30 cm)
Description: Slim, light-striped lizard with long, slender tail. Dark blotches on sides and throat.
Habitat: Chaparral, deserts and open forests throughout much of northern California.
Comments: Diurnal and often encountered. Moves in jerky steps, with head darting side to side.

WESTERN SKINK
Eumeces skiltonianus

Size: 2-3 in. (5-8 cm)
Description: Cylindrical, lizard-like creature has broad dorsal stripe edged in black. Juveniles have a blue tail.
Habitat: Woodlands and forests under ground litter.
Comments: Most active in the late afternoon. Like many lizards, its tail readily detaches when grasped by a predator; in such instances the detached tail wiggles, providing a diversion which often allows the tail-less skink to escape. The tail grows back in a few weeks.

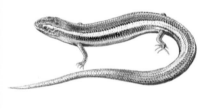

SIDE-BLOTCHED LIZARD
Uta stansburiana

Size: 4-7 in. (10-18 cm)
Description: Small brownish lizard with a blotched back and sides. Several variants exist, all of which have a prominent dark spot behind each front leg.
Habitat: Arid and semi-arid regions with rocky or sandy soil and low-growing plants.
Comments: Primarily ground-dwelling, it feeds on insects during the day.

WESTERN FENCE LIZARD
Sceloporous occidentalis

Size: 6-10 in. (15-25 cm)
Description: Spiny-scaled, brown-green or black lizard with blue patches on neck, sides and belly.
Habitat: Rocky areas, mixed forests, near buildings and fences.
Comments: Active during the day, it is often encountered. Will display blue undersides to attract females or defend territory.

SOUTHERN ALLIGATOR LIZARD
Gerrhonotus multicarinatus

Size: 10-17 in. (25-43 cm)
Description: Green to gray lizard with an elongate, stiff body, long tail and distinctive skin fold down each side.
Habitat: Found under ground litter in cool, moist woodlands.
Comments: Active during the day, it feeds largely on insects and snails. A good swimmer.

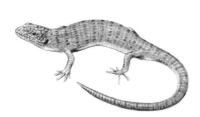

SNAKES

Snakes are limbless reptiles with moist, scaly skin, toothed jaws, no ear openings or eyelids and a single row of belly scales. They move by contracting their muscles in waves and undulating over the ground. All are carnivorous and swallow their prey whole. They flick their tongues in and out constantly to 'taste' and 'smell' the air around them. Most continue to grow in length during their life and shed their outer skin periodically. The vast majority are harmless to humans.

RACER
Coluber constrictor

Size: 2-6.5 ft. (60-200 cm)
Description: Slender green-brown snake with large eyes, a long tail and a yellow belly.
Habitat: Favors open areas including meadows, roadsides, prairies, forest glades, chaparral.
Comments: Active during the day, racers are fast-moving and good climbers. Often seen crossing roads. Holds its head and neck high when foraging.

COMMON KINGSNAKE
Lampropeltis getulus californiae

Size: 3-6 ft. (1-1.8 m)
Description: Large brown-black snake with light crossbands; light dorsal stripe may also be visible.
Habitat: Forests, rocky slopes, swamps, prairie, meadows, farmlands.
Comments: Active in mornings and afternoons, it hunts at night during hot weather. Diet consists of small mammals, rodents, lizards and snakes (including rattlers!).

WESTERN AQUATIC GARTER SNAKE
Thamnophis couchi

Size: 20-57 in. (50-145 cm)
Description: Six subspecies of this highly-variable snake are found in California. Most have a weak dorsal stripe and blotched sides. Others have distinct back and side stripes. All are aquatic and primarily diurnal.
Habitat: Rivers, streams and marshes throughout California.
Comments: Feeds on fish, amphibians and invertebrates.

CALIFORNIA RED-SIDED GARTER SNAKE
Thamnophis sirtalis infernalis

Size: 20-50 in. (50-127 cm)
Description: Dark snake with red blotches between its light dorsal and side stripes.
Habitat: Near water in meadows, farmlands and valleys.
Comments: Commonly encountered during the day. One of several subspecies of common garter snake, most of which have red blotches on the sides.

PACIFIC GOPHER SNAKE
Pituophis melanoleucus catenifer

Size: 3-8 ft. (1-2.5 m)
Description: Large, yellow-cream snake with dark blotches on its back and sides.
Habitat: Found in a variety of habitats (excluding swamps) from mountains to lowlands.
Comments: Though non-poisonous, it imitates a rattlesnake when threatened by coiling up, hissing loudly, vibrating its tail, and striking out at its aggressor. Eats primarily small rodents and is valued for pest control on farms.

WESTERN RATTLESNAKE
Crotalus viridis

Size: 1-5 ft. (30-150 cm)
Description: A darkly-blotched, greenish-brown snake with a flat head, defined neck and tail rattle.
Habitat: Grasslands, brushy areas and woodlands from sea level to 11,000 ft. (3,350 m).
Comments: A pit viper, it has heat sensing areas between its eyes and nostrils which help it detect prey. Enlarged front fangs have hollow canals which inject poison into prey when it strikes. Eats mostly rodents.

SALAMANDERS

Salamanders are smooth-skinned, tailed creatures that lack claws and ear openings. Some have the ability to regenerate tails or limbs lost to predators. Seldom seen, they live in dark, moist habitats and are nocturnal and secretive. They are most active in the spring and fall, especially near the pools where they breed.

Fertilization in most is internal but is not accomplished by copulation. During mating, the male releases a small packet of sperm which the female brushes against and draws into her body. The packet is kept in her body until she ovulates, which may be months later. Most species lay their eggs in water. Both adults and larvae are carnivorous and feed on worms and insects and other invertebrates.

CALIFORNIA NEWT
Taricha torosa

Size: 5-8 in. (13-20 cm)
Description: Warty skin is red-brown above, yellow to orange below. Breeding males have smooth skin.
Habitat: Near water in oak and pine woodlands.
Comments: When disturbed it assumes a defensive posture, exposing its brightly-colored undersides. Most likely to be seen on cool, wet days.

CALIFORNIA SLENDER SALAMANDER
Batrachoseps attenuatus

Size: 3-5 in. (8-13 cm)
Description: Blackish, worm-like salamander, has a yellow, red or brown dorsal stripe, tiny limbs and dark, white-speckled belly.
Habitat: Under moist leaf litter and logs in grasslands and woodlands.
Comments: The most common salamander in California. Easiest to spot during rainy weather.

CALIFORNIA TIGER SALAMANDER
Ambystoma tigrinum californiense

Size: 6-8 in. (15-20 cm)
Description: Black salamander covered in yellowish spots.
Habitat: Open woodlands and grasslands near water.
Comments: Most visible during breeding season from January-March.

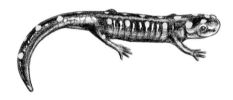

NORTHWESTERN SALAMANDER
Ambystoma gracile

Size: 4 in. (10 cm)
Description: Gray-brown salamander with a ridged tail and prominent swellings behind its eyes.
Habitat: Moist forests and grasslands.
Comments: A mole salamander, it spends much of its time underground feeding on worms, insects and small animals.

FROGS AND TOADS

Frogs and toads are squat amphibians common near ponds and lakes. All have large heads, large eyes, long hind legs and long, sticky tongues which they use to catch insects. Most have well-developed ears and strong voices. Only males are vocal.

Frogs have smooth skin, slim waists and many have prominent dorsal ridges. In most, the male initiates mating by calling for females. When he finds a mate, he clasps her in water and fertilizes the eggs as they are laid. The eggs initially hatch into fish-like tadpoles which breathe through gills and feed on vegetation. They later transform into young adults with limbs and lungs.

Toads can be distinguished from frogs by their dry, warty skin and prominent glands behind their eyes (parotoids). Some also have swellings between their eyes (bosses). When handled roughly by would-be predators, the warts and glands secrete a poisonous substance which makes the toads extremely unpalatable. Contrary to popular belief, handling toads does not cause warts.

PACIFIC TREEFROG
Hyla regilla

Size: 1-2 in. (2-5 cm)
Description: A dark green to tan frog, it is distinguished by its black eye stripe and large toe pads.
Habitat: Near water under shelter of grass or brush, from sea level to 10,000 ft. (3,000 m).
Comments: Largely nocturnal, it is the most commonly heard frog. Call is familiar to the movies, a high-pitched, two-part *kreck-ek*, the last syllable rising.

BULLFROG
Rana catesbeiana

Size: 4-8 in. (10-20 cm)
Description: Large green-brown frog with large ear openings.
Habitat: Ponds and lakes with ample vegetation.
Comments: Nocturnal, it is often seen along shorelines. Voice is a deep-pitched *jug-o-rum*. An introduced species.

RED-LEGGED FROG
Rana aurora

Size: 2-5 in. (5-13 cm)
Description: Olive-brown frog with a light jaw stripe, reddish groin and legs. Has well-developed folds of skin down its back.
Habitat: Damp, densely vegetated areas and woodlands.
Comments: Primarily diurnal. Call is a stuttering series of guttural growls lasting 2-3 seconds.

WESTERN SPADEFOOT TOAD
Scaphiopus hammondi

Size: 1-3 in. (3-8 cm)
Description: Brown-gray-green toad covered with random dark blotches. Skin covered in small bumps that are tipped in red or orange. Glossy, black wedge-shaped spade on each hind foot is used to excavate burrows.
Habitat: Grassy plains, gravelly flats.
Comments: Lives in deep burrows and is primarily nocturnal. Rolling call resembles a cat's purr.

CALIFORNIA TOAD
Bufo boreas halophilus

Size: 2-5 in. (5-13 cm)
Description: Gray-green toad with light dorsal stripe and warts framed by black blotches.
Habitat: Meadows, woodlands and valleys near water.
Comments: Call sounds like peeping chick. Nocturnal, it is active during the day in cooler weather.

WHAT ARE FISHES?

Fishes are cold-blooded vertebrates which are adapted to live in water and breathe through gills. They are characterized by their size, shape, feeding habits, and water temperature preference. Most live in either saltwater or freshwater, though a few species, such as salmon, divide their lives between the two.

All fishes have streamlined bodies covered in scales, and swim by flexing their bodies from side to side. The dorsal and anal fins act like keels, and the paired fins help to steer the fish and act as brakes. Many species possess an internal air bladder which acts as a depth regulator. By secreting gases into the bladder or absorbing gases from it, they are able to vary their body's density and control the level at which they swim.

Most fish reproduce by laying eggs freely in the water. In many, the male discharges sperm over the eggs as they are laid by the female. Depending on the species, eggs may float, sink, become attached to vegetation, or be buried. Survival rates tend to be largely influenced by environmental conditions.

HOW TO IDENTIFY FISHES

First, note the size, shape and color of the fish. Are there any distinguishing field marks like the double dorsal fins of the basses or the downturned lips of the suckers? Is the body thin or torpedo-shaped? Note the orientation and placement of fins on the body. Consult the text to confirm identification.

A trip to your local fish market or aquarium is a good way to hone your skills at identifying fish.

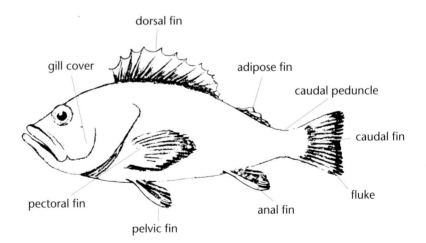

LAMPREYS

Lampreys are members of the most primitive order of fishes. All lack jaws and feed on the blood and tissue of other fishes.

PACIFIC LAMPREY
Lampetra tridentata

Size: To 30 in. (76 cm)
Description: Identified by its slender eel-like body, round gill openings and sucker-like mouth.
Habitat: Lampreys hatch in freshwater and spend their adult life in marine habitats.

Comments: Feeds by attaching itself by the mouth to host fishes, rasping a hole in their side with its horny teeth and sucking out nourishment.

SHARKS AND ALLIES

These fishes lack bones and have skeletons completely composed of cartilage. They also lack an internal air bladder and must swim continuously or sink to the bottom. Most live in marine environments.

SPINY DOGFISH
Squalus acanthias

Size: To 5 ft. (1.5 m)
Description: Gray-brown shark that lacks an anal fin and has a spine at the front of each dorsal fin. Sides often covered with light spots.
Habitat: Shallow water to depths of 120 ft. (36 m).
Comments: Very common in coastal waters and considered a pest by anglers.

LEOPARD SHARK
Triakis semifasciata

Size: To 6 ft. (2 m)
Description: Gray-brown shark with prominent dark spots.
Habitat: Common in shallow bays with sandy or rocky bottoms.

Comments: Often found in large schools, it is a popular food fish that is harvested commercially.

BAT RAY
Myliobatis californica
Size: To 6 ft. (1.8 m)
Description: Brown-green flat fish with a large, elevated head, long wings and a long, whip-like tail.
Habitat: Shallow waters with sandy bottoms.
Comments: Venomous stinger near base of tail can inflict a painful injury. A popular sport fish.

STURGEONS

Members of this prehistoric group are among the largest freshwater fishes in North America, reaching sizes to 20 ft. (6 m) and 3,200 lbs. (1,450 kg). Some live for up to 150 years.

WHITE STURGEON
Acipenser transmontanus
Size: To 10 ft. (3 m)
Description: Size and shape are key field marks. Note mouth barbels (whiskers).
Habitat: Feeds along the bottom in deep water.
Comments: These large fishes are found primarily in brackish water, though some move to the ocean. All spawn in fresh water.

HERRINGS AND ALLIES

Found in large schools, they are important forage and bait fishes.

PACIFIC HERRING
Clupea pallasii
Size: To 18 in. (46 cm)
Description: Greenish above, silvery below, with a short dorsal fin and a deeply-forked tail.
Habitat: Inshore waters.
Comments: Quantities of sticky eggs deposited on kelp and rocks during spawning are widely harvested for overseas markets.

NORTHERN ANCHOVY
Engraulis mordax

Size: To 9 in. (23 cm)
Description: Blue-green above, silvery below, with a snout projecting beyond the mouth.
Habitat: Nearshore waters, usually in dense schools.
Comments: Common bait fish that is harvested commercially for its meat and oil.

SALMON AND TROUT

This diverse group includes many popular sport fishes. Most have robust bodies, square caudal fins, an adipose fin and strong teeth. Trout are found primarily in fresh water; salmon are anadromous and live in saltwater for one or more years before returning to freshwater to spawn.

COHO SALMON
Oncorhynchus kisutch

Size: To 39 in. (1 m)
Description: Green-blue above, white below, with black spots on its back and the upper part of the caudal fin. Spawning males have bright red sides and dark bellies.
Habitat: Anadromous.
Comments: Also called silver salmon, they spend 2-3 years at sea before returning to spawn.

CHINOOK SALMON
Oncorhynchus tshawytscha

Size: To 58 in. (1.6 m)
Description: Blue-green above, it has irregular black spots on its back and on all of its caudal fin. Spawning males often have blotchy red sides.
Habitat: Anadromous.
Comments: The largest salmon, it weighs up to 92 lbs. (42 kg). Spawns in spring and fall and enters freshwater throughout the year. Also called king salmon.

SOCKEYE SALMON
Oncorhynchus nerka

Size: To 33 in. (84 cm)
Description: Blue-green above, it lacks dark spots on its back or fins. Spawning male has bright red body, green head, humped back and hooked jaw.
Habitat: Anadromous.
Comments: Formerly widespread, its spawning grounds are now limited to waters north of the Sacramento River.

CHUM SALMON
Oncorhynchus keta

Size: To 39 in. (1 m)
Description: This salmon lacks black spots and has a slender caudal peduncle. Distinguished from the sockeye by its white-edged lower fins. Spawning male has blotchy red sides.
Habitat: Anadromous.
Comments: Also called dog salmon, it spawns in streams close to the ocean in late fall and winter.

BROOK TROUT
Salvelinus fontinalis

Size: To 21 in. (53 cm)
Description: Colorful greenish fish with blue-haloed, red side spots and wavy light lines on back and dorsal fin. Lower fins are reddish.
Habitat: Clear, freshwater streams and rivers; some are anadromous.
Comments: An introduced sport fish weighing up to 14 lbs. (6.3 kg).

RAINBOW TROUT
Oncorhynchus mykiss

Size: To 45 in. (1.1 m)
Description: A silvery, dark-spotted fish named for the distinctive red-dish band running down its side. Band is most prominent during spring spawning.
Habitat: Abundant in streams, reservoirs and lakes.
Comments: Very important game fish. The sea-run version of this species is called steelhead.

BROWN TROUT
Salvelinus trutta

Size: To 39 in. (1 m)
Description: Brown fish covered with black and red spots.
Habitat: Cool streams and lakes; some are anadromous.
Comments: An introduced species renowned for its wariness.

GOLDEN TROUT
Oncorhynchus aguabonita

Size: To 28 in. (70 cm)
Description: Brilliantly-colored trout is dark above, yellow below, with bright red markings on its sides, belly and cheeks. Dorsal and caudal fins are covered with large, black spots.
Habitat: Primarily mountain lakes and streams.
Comments: California's state fish. Originally found in only the Kern River, it has been widely introduced throughout the state at high elevations.

MINNOWS AND ALLIES

These fishes can be distinguished from similar species by their lack of an adipose fin and toothless jaws. Lips are typically thin and tail is well-forked.

GOLDFISH
Carrasius auratus

Size: To 16 in. (40 cm)
Description: Thick gray-brown fish with large scales and a long dorsal fin.
Habitat: Sluggish streams, muddy ponds, sloughs.
Comments: Native to China, they are tolerant of warm and polluted waters. Domesticated goldfish are the more familiar orange color.

COMMON CARP
Cyprinus carpio

Size: To 48 in. (1.2 m)
Description: A large-scaled, deep-bodied olive fish, it is identified by its long dorsal fin, mouth barbels (whiskers) and forked, orangish tail. Dorsal fin has a single spine.
Habitat: Found in clear and turbid streams, ponds and sloughs. Prefers warm water.
Comments: Widely distributed throughout the U.S. Introduced to California.

CALIFORNIA ROACH
Hesperoleucus symmetricus

Size: To 4 in. (10 cm)
Description: Dull, dusky fish has a slightly subterminal mouth. Lips and fin bases are red-orange in mature fish. Tail is forked.
Habitat: Creeks, small rivers and tributaries.
Comments: Very common in coastal streams.

SPECKLED DACE
Rhinichthys osculus

Size: To 4 in. (10 cm)
Description: Highly variable, it is usually a dusky gray-olive fish with a black-speckled body and distinct side stripe.
Habitat: Pools, streams, rivers.
Comments: There are numerous subspecies of this widespread, common minnow.

GOLDEN SHINER
Notemigonus crysoleucas

Size: To 12 in. (30 cm)
Description: Deep-bodied, narrow fish with a silver-olive sides and light-colored fins. Often has a dark side stripe.
Habitat: Vegetated pools, streams, rivers and ponds.
Comments: Common bait fish often found in schools near the shore. A non-native species introduced throughout California.

SUCKERS

Suckers have distinctive, downturned fleshy lips that they use to 'vacuum' the bottom of lakes and streams in search of invertebrates.

SACRAMENTO SUCKER
Catostomus occidentalis

Size: To 24 in. (60 cm)
Description: Brown-green above, yellowish below with downturned lips. Breeding male has a reddish side stripe.
Habitat: Clear pools, streams, lakes.
Comments: Unlike many bottom-feeding fishes, suckers lack mouth barbels.

CODFISHES

All have long tapering bodies and long dorsal and anal fins. Barbels are often present.

PACIFIC HAKE
Merluccius productus

Size: To 3 ft. (90 cm)
Description: Elongate silvery fish with jutting lower jaw and sharp teeth. Second dorsal and anal fins are notched.
Habitat: Open sea from surface to depths of 3,000 ft. (914 m).
Comments: Often caught by anglers trolling for salmon.

LIVEBEARERS

Livebearers are fertilized internally and give birth to live young.

MOSQUITOFISH
Gambusia affinis

Size: To 2.5 in. (6 cm)
Description: Olive-brown above, yellowish below with 1-3 rows of dark spots on dorsal fin and tail.
Habitat: Fresh- and saltwater ponds, lakes, slow-moving streams.
Comments: Feed on mosquito larvae and have been widely introduced throughout California.

STICKLEBACKS

These small fishes are named for the defined row of spines along their back. Noted for their mating behavior, the males are responsible for building intricate, suspended nests and guarding the eggs and young.

THREESPINE STICKLEBACK
Gasterosteus aculeatus

Size: To 4 in. (10 cm)
Description: Slender green fish distinguished by the row of 3 short spines ahead of the dorsal fin.
Habitat: Found in shallow, vegetated streams, pools and small lakes.
Comments: Diet consists of crustaceans, insects and algae.

TEMPERATE BASSES

Found in fresh- and saltwater, they are important commercial and sport fishes.

STRIPED BASS
Morone saxatilis

Size: To 6 ft. (1.8 m)
Description: Olive to blue-gray
fish with 6-9 dark side stripes.
Habitat: Nearshore waters.
Comments: Introduced to the
west coast in the late 1800s, it is
now widespread and common.

SUNFISHES

Members all have two joined dorsal fins separated by a notch. Popular sport fishes, they have been widely introduced throughout California.

LARGEMOUTH BASS
Micropterus salmoides

Size: To 39 in. (1 m)
Description: Greenish, mottled
fish with a dark, often blotched,
side stripe. Upper jaw extends
beyond the eye.
Habitat: Quiet, vegetated lakes,
ponds and rivers.
Comments: A very popular
sport fish that is taken with live
and artificial bait. The similar
smallmouth bass has blotched
sides and its jaw does not extend
beyond the eye.

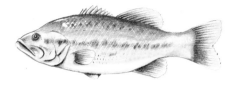

BLUEGILL
Lepomis macrochirus

Size: To 16 in. (40 cm)
Description: Flattened brassy fish
with long pectoral fins and a dark-
spotted dorsal fin. Side bars are
usually visible. Body color ranges
from blue to yellow.
Habitat: Quiet, vegetated lakes,
ponds and rivers.
Comments: One of the most popular
panfishes in the country.

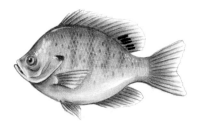

BLACK CRAPPIE
Pomoxis nigromaculatus

Size: To 16 in. (40 cm)
Description: Greenish, mottled fish with a hunched back. Dorsal fin is set well back and has 7-8 spines.
Habitat: Quiet, clear lakes, ponds and rivers.
Comments: Another non-native species that has been widely introduced in California. The similar white crappie has 6 dorsal spines.

JACKS

A diverse family of mostly streamlined, fast-moving fishes with a deeply forked tails.

YELLOWTAIL
Seriola lalandi

Size: To 5 ft. (1.5 m)
Description: A large, silvery fish with a yellowish side stripe and yellow, forked tail.
Habitat: Offshore waters.
Comments: One of California's most popular sport fishes, up to 400,000 are taken by anglers annually.

SURFPERCHES

Flattened fishes with a long dorsal fin. Several species are frequently caught by surf anglers along the coast.

STRIPED SEAPERCH
Embiotoca lateralis

Size: To 14 in. (36 cm)
Description: A colorful fish told by its blue and orange side stripes.
Habitat: Offshore waters.
Comments: Over 100,000 are taken annually by anglers and spearfishers.

DAMSELFISHES

Family of nearshore fishes that are often brightly-colored.

GARIBALDI
Hypsypops rubicundus

Size: To 14 in. (36 cm)
Description: Bright orange fish
with a deeply-notched tail.
Habitat: Nearshore waters from
Monterey Bay south.
Comments: It is illegal to spear or
retain this protected species
in California.

WRASSES

Family of colorful, buck-toothed tropical fishes.

CALIFORNIA SHEEPHEAD
Semicossyphus pulcher

Size: To 3 ft. (90 cm)
Description: Told by black
head and rear, red middle
and white chin.
Habitat: Shallow waters in
southern California.
Comments: Common along
rocky shores.

BARRACUDAS

Slender, silvery fishes with two widely-spaced dorsal fins and long snouts.

CALIFORNIA BARRACUDA
Sphyraena argentea

Size: To 4 ft. (1.2 m)
Description: Slender blue-gray
or brown fish with a long snout,
jutting lower jaw and
prominent teeth.
Habitat: Offshore waters to
depth of 60 ft. (18 m).
Comments: A prized sport fish
that is also harvested commercially.

MACKERELS

Family of fast-swimming fishes with torpedo-shaped bodies and pointed snouts. Many are important commercially.

PACIFIC MACKEREL
Scomber japonicus

Size: To 25 in. (64 cm)
Description: Dark blue to green above, silvery below with numerous, black bars down its back.
Habitat: Nearshore waters to 50 miles offshore.
Comments: Swims in large schools and is common in nearshore waters. An excellent food fish.

PACIFIC BONITO
Sarda chiliensis

Size: To 40 in. (1 m)
Description: Green-blue above, silvery below with dark, oblique stripes on body.
Habitat: Nearshore waters to 30 miles offshore.
Comments: Swims in schools and is a prized sport fish.

ROCKFISHES

Most members of this large family have prominent, spiky dorsal fins and large eyes. Spines of the dorsal, anal and pelvic fins are venomous and can cause painful injury.

VERMILLION ROCKFISH
Sebastes miniatus

Size: To 30 in. (76 cm)
Description: Reddish above, light red or orange below with red fins. Older individuals have gray marks on their head and back.
Habitat: Shallow to deep rocky reefs.
Comments: Often caught by anglers, it is an excellent food fish.

BLACK-AND-YELLOW ROCKFISH
Sebastes chrysomelas

Size: To 15 in. (38 cm)
Description: Black-and-yellow blotched rockfish.
Habitat: Nearshore water to depths of 120 ft. (37 m).
Comments: Valued food fish often found near kelp beds.

GREENLINGS

Fishes with long bodies and long dorsal and anal fins.

LINGCOD
Ophiodon elongatus

Size: To 5 ft. (1.5 m)
Description: Large green-brown fish with a jutting lower jaw and a long, spiny, notched dorsal fin.
Habitat: Nearshore waters.
Comments: Very important commercial and sport fish.

FLATFISHES

Flattened fishes with both eyes on the same side of the body. They often lie on the bottom buried in sediment with only their eyes exposed.

CALIFORNIA HALIBUT
Paralichthys californicus

Size: To 5 ft. (1.5 m)
Description: Flat fish with long dorsal and anal fins.
Habitat: Offshore waters.
Comments: Related to numerous similar species of flatfishes found off the California coast. An important commercial and sport fish.

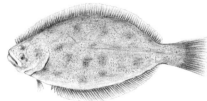

WHAT IS SEASHORE LIFE?

This section includes a variety of animal and plant groups that can be found along the west coast of California. Most species can be readily observed in tidal pools or shallow waters. All of the animals in this section are classed as invertebrates or 'animals without backbones.'

The best time to observe the greatest variety of species is during low tide. Tide times are often published in newspapers, and tide tables are available at most sporting goods stores. There are generally two tides a day, and tidal differences may be as much as 15 ft. (4.5 m). The lowest tides of the year occur in midwinter and midsummer.

The groups covered in this section include marine plants, coelenterates, sea stars and allies, crustaceans and mollusks.

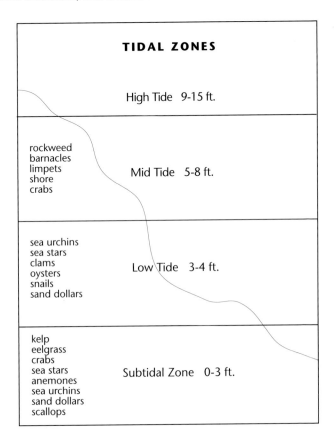

TIDAL ZONES

High Tide   9-15 ft.

rockweed
barnacles
limpets
shore
crabs

Mid Tide   5-8 ft.

sea urchins
sea stars
clams
oysters
snails
sand dollars

Low Tide   3-4 ft.

kelp
eelgrass
crabs
sea stars
anemones
sea urchins
sand dollars
scallops

Subtidal Zone   0-3 ft.

MARINE PLANTS

This general group includes a few of the most common coastal marine plants.

BULL KELP
Nereocystis luetkeana

Size: To 65 ft. (20 m)
Description: Long, tubular stem is anchored to the bottom and supported by a round float. Long, bladed, brownish 'leaves' radiate away from the float along the water's surface.
Habitat: Found in dense beds along shorelines to depths of 100 ft. (30 m).
Comments: Kelp beds provide an important source of food and cover for invertebrates, fishes and mammals.

ROCKWEED
Fucus distichus

Size: To 20 in. (50 cm)
Description: A ragged, brownish plant with swollen air bladders along a ribbed stem.
Habitat: Rocky shorelines.
Comments: Very widely-distributed.

EELGRASS
Zostera marina

Size: To 5 ft. (1.5 m)
Description: Tall slender plant with grass-like leaves.
Habitat: Muddy and sandy soils.
Comments: Leaves are often encrusted with animals and insects. Surfgrass (*Phylospadix*) is more common than eelgrass south of Santa Barbara.

SEA PALM
Postelsia palmaeformis

Size: To 24 in. (60 cm)
Description: Resembles a palm tree with drooping leaves.
Habitat: Intertidal.
Comments: Sea palm, eelgrass and surfgrass all have special protection under the animal-oriented Fish and Game Code.

COELENTERATES

This group contains a variety of free-swimming and colonial creatures including jellyfish, hydroids, anemones and corals.

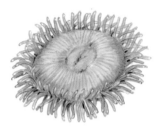

GIANT GREEN ANEMONE
Anthopleura xanthogrammica

Size: To 10 in. (25 cm)
Description: Flattened green disk with numerous, uniform tentacles.
Habitat: Very common in tide pools on exposed shores.
Comments: Algae living in the tissues of the animal are responsible for its color.

BROODING ANEMONE
Epiactis prolifera

Size: To 2 in. (5 cm)
Description: Identified by its flower-like profile. Color ranges from red-pink to green.
Habitat: Commonly found at low tide attached to eelgrass and rocks.
Comments: Terminal mouth is surrounded by up to 90 stinging tentacles which are withdrawn when disturbed.

MOON JELLYFISH
Aurelia aurita

Size: To 16 in. (40 cm)
Description: Told by white, translucent, bell-shaped body with fringe of numerous, stinging tentacles.
Habitat: Found floating on the surface of the water or washed ashore.
Comments: Stings can cause an itchy rash. Like all jellyfish, it swims by expelling water from its mouth.

SEA STARS AND ALLIES

These mostly bottom-dwelling animals are characterized by spiny bodies and radial symmetry, i.e., body parts repeat around a central hub, as in a wheel. The 'arms' are usually arranged in multiples of 5, and may be short or long, cylindrical or flattened.

OCHRE SEA STAR
Pisaster ochraceus

Size: To 14 in. (35 cm)
Description: Identified by its short rays and patterned surface. Body color may be purple, yellow, orange or brown.
Habitat: Common in tidepools and attached to rocks at low tide.
Comments: Like most sea stars, it is capable of regenerating severed body parts.

GIANT SPINED SEA STAR
Pisaster giganteus

Size: To 2 ft. (60 cm)
Description: Large sea star may be red, brown tan or purple. Delicate spines have blue rings around their base.
Habitat: Found on rocks during low tides.
Comments: Although sea stars have no jaws, most are carnivorous and very destructive to shellfish populations.

PURPLE SEA URCHIN
Strongylocentrotus purpuatus

Size: To 4 in. (10 cm)
Description: Told at a glance by its red-purple color, rounded body and long spines.
Habitat: Rocky shores below the low tide line.
Comments: Is commercially harvested for its gonads which are considered a sushi delicacy in Japan.

SAND DOLLAR
Dendraster excentricus

Size: To 4 in. (10 cm)
Description: Hard brown body is covered with short spines. Note flower-like impression on shell.
Habitat: Found at low tides on sandy beaches, often partially buried.
Comments: Shells of dead sand dollars are often found washed up on beaches.

CRUSTACEANS

Like insects, crustaceans have a hard external skeleton, antennae and paired limbs. The limbs differ greatly in form and function, and are modified for specific purposes in different species. Most live in water.

PURPLE SHORE CRAB
Hemigrapsus nudas

Size: To 2 in. (5 cm)
Description: Distinguished by its deep purple body and red-spotted claws. Red-brown, green and yellow variants also exist.
Habitat: Beneath rocks in protected waters.
Comments: Often found scuttling about on intertidal rocks.

DUNGENESS CRAB
Cancer magister

Size: To 12 in. (30 cm)
Description: Large red-brown crab.
Habitat: Young are found in sandy pools near low-tide line; older individuals gradually migrate into deeper waters.
Comments: This is the crab often found in markets. Though locally abundant, there is some concern that populations are being over-fished.

ACORN BARNACLE
Balanus glandula

Size: To 1 in. (2.5 cm)
Description: A small white-gray,
heavily-ribbed shell that often grows
in clusters attached to rocks and piers
at the high tide line.
Habitat: Very common throughout
coastal California.
Comments: Barnacles hatch as free-
swimming larvae which eventually
attach themselves to solid objects
and mature into shelled adults. They
feed by opening plates at the top of
their shells and extending feathery
arms to trap small organisms.

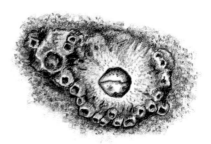

GOOSENECK BARNACLE
Lepas anatifera

Size: To 2 in. (5 cm)
Description: Flexible stalk topped
with 5 hard whitish plates.
Habitat: Widely distributed in the
intertidal zone.
Comments: Often found in clusters
attached to floating objects.

MOLLUSKS

This large group of soft-bodied and usually hard-shelled invertebrates
occupies many habitats in water and on land. The mouth of most
mollusks – excluding bivalves – has a ribbon-like toothed structure called
a radula which helps the animals break down food or capture prey.

ROUGH KEYHOLE LIMPET
Diodera aspera

Size: To 2 in. (5 cm)
Description: Cone-shaped shell has
side ribs and a hole in the top.
Habitat: Found intertidally on kelp
and rocks.
Comments: Color of shell ranges
from white to tan and gray and is
influenced by the kinds of animals
that colonize the shell surface.

BLACK TURBAN SNAIL
Tegula funebralis

Size: To 1.5 in. (4 cm)
Description: Thick, purplish-black shell houses a black snail.
Habitat: Abundant at low tides on exposed shores.
Comments: Limpets often attach themselves to its shell to feed off the algae that collect there.

CALIFORNIA HORN SNAIL
Cerithidea californica

Size: To 1.2 in. (3 cm)
Description: Stout, spire-like shell has 10-11 whorls. Color is usually brown, though some are almost black.
Habitat: Mud flats.
Comments: Very common on mud flats when the tide is out.

BLACK ABALONE
Haliotis cracherodii

Size: To 5-8 in. (13-20 cm)
Description: Large, oval shell is black, blue or green. Interior is pearly white.
Habitat: High-tide mark to 20 ft. (6 m) depth.
Comments: Though abundant, it has little commercial value. Its larger cousin, the red abalone (*Haliotis refescens*), is the species typically served in local restaurants.

NATIVE LITTLENECK CLAM
Protothaca staminea

Size: To 3 in. (8 cm)
Description: Rounded, white shell is ribbed with growth lines.
Habitat: Sandy and gravelly soils in the mid-tide region.
Comments: Feeds by extracting minute particles from the water passing over its gills.

PACIFIC OYSTER
Crassostrea gigas

Size: To 12 in. (30 cm)
Description: Distinguished at a glance by its heavy, irregular shell.
Habitat: Common in the intertidal zone.
Comments: Like other bivalves (including clams, mussels and scallops), its body is composed of two hinged shells held together by powerful muscles. Most live in sand or mud.

CALIFORNIA MUSSEL
Mytilus californianus

Size: To 10 in. (25 cm)
Description: Thick, oval-shaped, blue-black shell has prominent ridges.
Habitat: Intertidal waters, rock crevices.
Comments: Very abundant along rocky coasts.

BLUE MUSSEL
Mytilus edulis

Size: To 2 in. (5 cm)
Description: Blue-black shell is oval-shaped and relatively smooth.
Habitat: Intertidal waters.
Comments: Common on exposed shores. Often found attached to pilings and other marine objects.

PACIFIC PINK SCALLOP
Chlamys hastata

Size: To 3 in. (8 cm)
Description: Beautiful fan-shaped shell is often covered with colored sponges and may be white, yellow, orange, purple or pink.
Habitat: Intertidal waters.
Comments: Unlike other bivalves, scallops possess a set of eyes that line the edge of the shell.

WHAT ARE TREES AND SHRUBS?

TREES

Trees can be broadly defined as perennial woody plants at least 16 ft. (5 m) tall with a single stem and a well-developed crown of branches, twigs and leaves. Most are long-lived plants and range in age from 40-50 years for smaller deciduous trees to several hundred years for many of the conifers.

A tree's size and shape is largely determined by its genetic makeup, but growth is also affected by environmental factors such as moisture, light and competition from other species. Trees growing in crowded stands will often only support compact crowns, due to the competition for light. Some species at high altitudes grow gnarled and twisted as a result of exposure to high winds.

SHRUBS

Shrubs are perennial woody plants normally less than 16 ft. (5 m) tall that support a crown of branches, twigs and leaves. Unlike trees, they are anchored to the ground by several stems rather than a single trunk. Most are fast-growing and provide an important source of food and shelter for wildlife.

N.B. – Some shrubs that are most conspicuous when in bloom are included in the following section on flowering plants.

HOW TO IDENTIFY TREES AND SHRUBS

First, note its size and shape. Does it have one or several 'trunks.' Examine the size, color, and shape of the leaves and how they are arranged on the twigs. Are they opposite or alternate? Simple or compound? Hairy or smooth? Are flowers or fruits visible on branches or on the ground? Once you've collected as much information as you can, consult the illustrations and text to confirm your sighting.

LEAF ARRANGEMENTS

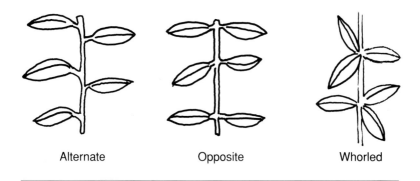

Alternate   Opposite   Whorled

LEAF SHAPES

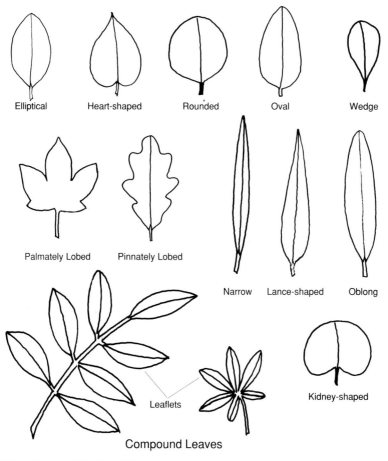

Elliptical   Heart-shaped   Rounded   Oval   Wedge

Palmately Lobed   Pinnately Lobed

Narrow   Lance-shaped   Oblong

Leaflets

Kidney-shaped

Compound Leaves

YEWS

Yews are a primitive race of needle-leaved evergreen trees that lack woody cones.

CALIFORNIA TORREYA
Torreya californica

Size: 20-80 ft. (6-24 m)
Description: Stiff, evergreen leaves are flattened with a sharp tip and grow in two rows along twigs. Plum-like fruit contains a large brown seed.
Habitat: Mixed evergreen forests and exposed slopes in northen California.
Comments: This highly aromatic tree is also called the 'stinking cedar' due to the offensive odor released when its leaves are crushed.

PINES

Most have long, needle-like leaves which grow grouped in bundles of two to five. Male and female cones usually occur on the same tree.

LODGEPOLE PINE
Pinus contorta

Size: 65-130 ft. (20-40 m)
Description: Crown is ragged and slender, straight trunk is often barren when shaded. Stiff needles are twisted into bundles of two and cone scales have a single prickle near their outer edge.
Habitat: Bogs, alpine forests, sandy soils.
Comments: Named for its straight trunk which Native Americans used for teepee poles. Cones are stimulated to open by heat and this is often one of the first trees to reseed burned-out areas.

WESTERN WHITE PINE
Pinus monticola

Size: 50-165 ft. (15-50 m)
Description: Straight trunk supports a ragged, conical crown of horizontally growing branches. Blue-green needles are arranged in clusters of five. Long-stalked, elongate cones are up to 15 in. (38 cm) long.
Habitat: Found in mixed and pure stands in the northern Sierra Nevada mountains.
Comments: One of the largest pines, its wood is highly desirable since it is of a uniformly high grade.

BRISTLECONE PINE
Pinus aristata

Size: 20-60 ft. (6-18 m)
Description: Tree with needles arranged into tight bundles of five that grow curved around the twig. Purplish cones bristle with stiff, recurved prickles.
Habitat: Dry, rocky exposed slopes in eastern California.
Comments: The oldest living trees on earth with some specimens over 4,500 years old. Found in the Inyo National Forest.

PONDEROSA PINE
Pinus ponderosa

Size: 50-130 ft. (15-39 m)
Description: Stout, stiff needles are up to eight inches (20 cm) long and grouped in bundles of two or three. Oval cones have scales that terminate in sharp prickles.
Habitat: Widespread in mountain regions, usually in pure stands.
Comments: Very common and an important timber tree. Most common at elevations between 3,000-5,000 ft. (900-1,500 m).

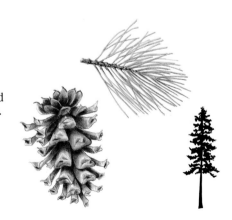

SUGAR PINE
Pinus lambertiana

Size: 100-200 ft. (30-60 m)
Description: Sharply pointed blue-green needles are bundled in fives. Elongate, stalked cones are 12-24 in. (30-60 cm) long.
Habitat: Mixed coniferous forests.
Comments: The largest American pine, it is named for its sweet sap. Trunks may be up to 10 ft. (3 m) in diameter.

SINGLELEAF PINYON PINE
Pinus monophylla

Size: 15-30 ft. (4.5-9 m)
Description: Small, often shrubby, pine with spreading, rounded branches. Stiff needles grow singly along twigs. Short-stalked, rounded cones produce large seeds that are sold as pine nuts.
Habitat: Dry, gravelly and rocky soils.
Comments: Is one of four species of pinyon pines found in the south-western states.

FIRS

Firs are medium-sized evergreens with dense crowns. Flattened, stalkless needles grow singly and bear a longitudinal scar from base to tip. Cones grow upright from branches and disintegrate when seeds are ripe. After the cone scales are shed, a central, candle-like stalk remains on the branch.

WHITE FIR
Abies concolor

Size: 100-160 ft. (30-48 m)
Description: Flexible needles are flat and blunt-tipped and grow to the sides or curve upward. Cylindrical cones are green, purple or yellow and up to five inches (13 cm) long.
Habitat: Moist soils in pure or mixed stands with other firs.
Comments: An important food source for deer, grouse, porcupines, rodents and birds. Firs often have symmetrical crowns and are prized Christmas ornamentals.

DOUGLAS-FIRS

Larger than true firs, Douglas-firs are easily identified by their shaggy cones.

DOUGLAS-FIR
Pseudotsuga menziesii

Size: 100-250 ft. (30-75 m)
Description: Flexible needles grow along twigs that terminate in red buds. Cones are distinguished at a glance by the three-pointed bracts protruding between scales. Side branches in the crown droop.
Habitat: Moist, well-drained soils from sea level to 9,000 ft. (2,750 m).
Comments: One of the tallest and most important timber trees in the U.S.

REDWOODS AND ALLIES

The large size of these famous trees is attributed to their resistance to disease, fire and insects. Both the redwood and sequoia are found primarily in California.

REDWOOD
Sequoia sempervirens

Size: 200-300 ft. (60-92 m)
Description: A very tall tree with a straight trunk, red-brown fibrous bark and an open, irregular crown. Trunk diameter is typically 10-15 ft. (3-5 m). Tiny cones are one inch (3 cm) long.
Habitat: Moist soils and bottomlands in the coastal fog belt.
Comments: The world's tallest tree is also California's state tree. Once widespread, surviving members are now protected in a number of national and state parks.

GIANT SEQUOIA
Sequoiadendron giganteum

Size: 150-250 ft. (45-75 m)
Description: Huge thick-trunked tree with fibrous red bark. Scale-like leaves are tightly bunched along twigs. Trunk is deeply furrowed at base.
Habitat: Rocky soils at elevations above 4,500 ft. (1,370 m) in central California.
Comments: Considered the largest trees on earth (in mass), exceptional specimens are over 270 ft. (82 m) tall and 3,800 years old.

CEDARS AND ALLIES

All have scaly or awl-shaped leaves which are tightly bunched together on twigs. The heavily-weighted twigs usually droop at their tips and give the plants a relaxed profile. Most cedar wood is very fragrant.

INCENSE CEDAR
Calocedrus decurrens

Size: 50-150 ft. (15-45 m)
Description: Large tree with fibrous, brown bark. Long, scale-like leaves are arranged in small, vase-shaped whorls along twigs, lumpy to the touch. Oblong cones are composed of six flattened scales that open when ripe.
Habitat: Mountain slopes between 1,000-8,000 ft. (300-2,400 m).
Comments: An aromatic tree, it is an important source of timber for siding, shakes, chests and pencils.

MONTEREY CYPRESS
Cupressus macrocarpa

Size: 50-80 ft. (15-24 m)
Description: Picturesque coastal tree has a flat-topped, irregular crown and twisted trunk in exposed areas. Scale-like leaves have blunt tips.
Habitat: Exposed coastal headlands.
Comments: Young trees growing in protected areas have symmetrical crowns. Native to the Monterey Bay region, it has been widely introduced throughout California.

CALIFORNIA JUNIPER
Juniperus californica

Size: To 40 ft. (12 m)
Description: Shrub or small tree with a branching, irregular crown. Scale-like needles grow in threes along twigs. Bluish, berry-like fruits are often conspicuous.
Habitat: Dry slopes throughout the mountains and foothills, semi-desert areas.
Comments: In desert regions, it is often associated with pinyon pines and Joshua trees.

WILLOWS AND ALLIES

Most have narrow, finely-toothed leaves which grow alternately along twigs. Flowers often appear in spring before the leaves along semi-erect catkins. After pollination, flowers are succeeded by small pods. When ripe, these pods burst open and shed numerous 'cottony' seeds in the wind.

ARROYO WILLOW
Salix lasiolepis

Size: To 30 ft. (9 m)
Description: Shrub or small tree with an irregular crown of erect branches. Lance-shaped, long leaves are finely-toothed
Habitat: Wet soils along arroyos (gulches, gullies) and streams.
Comments: Noted for their extensive root systems, willows are often instrumental in preventing soil erosion along stream banks.

WEEPING WILLOW
Salix babylonica

Size: To 50 ft. (15 m)
Description: Easily distinguished by its short trunk and wide crown of drooping (weeping) branches. Narrow, finely-toothed leaves are evident from early spring until late autumn.
Habitat: Moist soils, along streams.
Comments: Native to China, this introduced willow is widely planted as an ornamental throughout California.

POPLARS

Found in moist habitats, these fast-growing trees are distinguished from willows by their drooping flower clusters (catkins). Alternate, unlobed leaves are toothed, generally heart-shaped and usually as long as they are broad. Green-white bark of young trees becomes grayish and furrowed as it matures.

FREMONT COTTONWOOD
Populus fremontii

Size: 50-80 ft. (15-24 m)
Description: Has a large, broad crown of spreading branches. Heart-shaped leaves have gently-toothed edges and flattened stems. Reddish flowers bloom in drooping catkins and are succeeded by capsules containing cotton seeds.
Habitat: Wet soils near water.
Comments: In dry areas, cottonwoods indicate the presence of underground water.

TREMBLING ASPEN
Populus tremuloides

Size: To 100 ft. (33 m)
Description: Long, slender trunk supports a crown of spreading branches. Rounded leaves have long stems and the leaves rustle (tremble) in the slightest breeze. Leaves turn yellow in autumn.
Habitat: Well-drained soils in a variety of situations.
Comments: Its twigs, leaves, catkins and bark are an important food source for wildlife.

LOMBARDY POPLAR
Populus nigra

Size: 30-80 ft. (9-24 m)
Description: Distinguished by its narrow crown of short, erect branches. Leaves are roughly triangular.
Habitat: Moist soils.
Comments: Introduced from Europe, it is now widely planted throughout California as an ornamental.

BIRCHES

Leaves are commonly oval-shaped with toothed margins. Distinctive, cylindrical, woody cones (strobiles) disintegrate in the fall when ripe. All are fast-growing and short-lived.

EUROPEAN WHITE BIRCH
Betula pendula

Size: To 60 ft. (18 m)
Description: Distinguished by its crown of drooping branches. Leaves are rounded-triangular with toothed margins. Bark is papery and peels off in strips.
Habitat: Moist soils.
Comments: Grows rapidly and planted throughout California.

ALDERS

Alders are fast-growing shrubs and trees with ragged crowns and deeply veined leaves. Their fruit is a distinctive woody cone.

WHITE ALDER
Alnus rhombifolia

Size: To 80 ft. (24 m)
Description: Tree with a rounded crown of spreading branches. Alternate leaves are saw-toothed and up to four inches (10 cm) long.
Habitat: Near streams to 8,000 ft. (2,400 m) elevation.
Comments: Easily distinguished in winter when yellow male catkins dangle from leafless twigs.

OAKS

Oaks represent a group of important hardwoods. Generally, they are large trees with stout trunks and spreading crowns that produce acorns for fruit.

CALIFORNIA WHITE OAK
Quercus lobata

Size: 60-120 ft. (18-37 m)
Description: Large tree with a stout trunk and widely spreading branches. Leaves have 7-11 rounded lobes and are up to four inches (10 cm) long. Acorns are slim and conical.
Habitat: Rich soils in valleys and foothills.
Comments: Common throughout California's interior and central coast range, its acorns are a valuable source of food for birds and mammals.

CALIFORNIA BLACK OAK
Quercus kelloggii

Size: 40-90 ft. (12-27 m)
Description: Large tree with a round crown. Leaves have five to seven deeply-toothed lobes and are up to six inches (15 cm) long. Rounded acorns have a scaly cup.
Habitat: Dry, well-drained soils in foothills and mountains.
Comments: Leaves distinguish it from other oaks. Popular source of firewood.

CALIFORNIA LIVE OAK
Quercus agrifolia

Size: 30-90 ft. (9-27 m)
Description: Evergreen with a spreading crown of branches and a stout trunk. Leaves are oblong and arched upward. Acorns are conical.
Habitat: Slopes and valleys.
Comments: The common oak along the coast.

CALIFORNIA SCRUB OAK
Quercus dumosa

Size: To 10 ft. (3 m)
Description: Shrub or small tree with small, oval, evergreen leaves. Acorns have a thick, scaly cup.
Habitat: Dry, barren areas.
Comments: A major component of the chaparral community, it often grows in thickets.

LAURELS

Mostly aromatic trees and shrubs providing camphor, cinnamon, and aromatic oils.

CALIFORNIA LAUREL
Umbellularia californica

Size: 40-80 ft. (12-24 m)
Description: Tree with short trunk supporting large rounded crown. Narrow leathery leaves exude a spicy scent when crushed. Clusters of yellow spring flowers are succeeded by greenish-purple berries that ripen in autumn.
Habitat: Moist, fertile soils from sea level to 6,000 ft. (1,800 m).
Comments: Commonly planted as an ornamental tree along the coast.

SYCAMORES

Large trees with very stout trunks and distinctive 'buttonball' fruits.

CALIFORNIA SYCAMORE
Platanus racemosa

Size: 40-90 ft. (12-27 m)
Description: Massive trunk supports broad crown of spreading branches. The bark flakes off in irregular patches and it appears white-brown at a glance. Leaves have five lobes and are somewhat star-shaped. Fruit consists of a ball of numerous seeds supported on stiff upright hairs.
Habitat: Moist soils along streams in valleys and canyons.
Comments: One of three sycamores native to the U.S.

ROSES AND ALLIES

A variable family of trees and shrubs found throughout North America.

BITTER CHERRY
Prunus emarginata

Size: To 40 ft. (12 m)
Description: Leaves are oval or lance-shaped and taper to a point. White flowers bloom in spring in round, flat-topped clusters and are succeeded by small, bright red berries.
Habitat: Found in dry to moist soil in coastal region and Sierra Nevada.
Comments: The fruit is extremely bitter and not edible.

MOUNTAIN MAHOGANY
Cercocarpus betuloides

Size: To 25 ft. (7.5 m)
Description: Shrub or small tree with a spreading crown. Toothed, evergreen leaves are elliptical with a narrow base. Yellowish flowers are succeeded by fruits with a feathery plume at the tip.
Habitat: Dry mountain slopes, chaparral.
Comments: The term *cercocarpus* is derived from the Greek words for 'tail' and 'fruit.'

TOYON
Heteromeles arbutifolia

Size: To 30 ft. (9 m)
Description: A beautiful tree or shrub with a short trunk and a spreading, round crown. Thick, oblong, evergreen leaves are sharply-toothed. White flowers bloom in dense clusters in early summer and are succeeded in autumn by small, red apple-like fruits.
Habitat: Slopes, canyons and streamsides to 4,000 ft. (1,200 m).
Comments: Fruits persist into winter and are very showy.

CHAMISE
Adenostoma fasciculatum

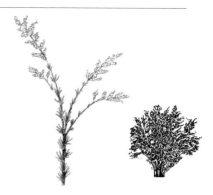

Size: 3-7 ft. (2-3 m)
Description: Wiry shrub or small tree with dark brown, shredding bark and bundled, needle-like leaves. Clusters of tiny white flowers bloom at stem tips in spring.
Habitat: Chaparral, foothills.
Comments: Also called greasewood for its oily, stringy wood.

PEAS & ALLIES

Most members of this large family of trees, shrubs and herbs produce fruit in seed pods.

HONEY MESQUITE
Prosopis glandulosa

Size: To 20 ft. (6 m)
Description: Shrub or small tree with crown of crooked branches. Leaves are up to 10 in. (25 cm) long and have 7-20 pairs of leaflets. Distinctive fruit is narrow pod.
Habitat: Grasslands, sandy soils, deserts.
Comments: Wood is an excellent source of firewood, charcoal and fence posts. Named for its sweet seeds that native Indians used in cakes and fermented drinks.

CALTROP FAMILY

Family of shrubs, herbs and trees found in hot climates.

CREOSOTE BUSH
Larrea tridentata

Size: To 10 ft. (3 m)
Description: One of the most common desert shrubs, it is told by its twisted, grayish stems and sparse foliage. Small yellow flowers (.5 in./ 1 cm) bloom throughout the year.
Habitat: Well drained soils in deserts to elevations of 5,000 ft. (1,500 m).
Comments: The plant exudes a pungent odor following desert rains.

BUCKTHORNS
Family of woody shrubs and trees with over 700 species worldwide.

BLUEBLOSSOM
Ceanothus thyrsiflorus

Size: To 20 ft. (6 m)
Description: Shrub or small tree with branching clusters of showy, blue flowers. Green bark reddens with age.
Habitat: Coastal mountains, chaparral, mixed forests, roadsides.
Comments: Flowers are fragrant and reminiscent of lilacs.

BUCKEYES
Named for their dark-brown seeds that each have a light 'eye' spot.

CALIFORNIA BUCKEYE
Aesculus californica

Size: To 30 ft. (9 m)
Description: Shrub or small tree. Leaves have five to seven pointed leaflets. Pinkish flowers bloom in erect clusters in late spring. Fruits have one or two seeds.
Habitat: Moist soils, canyons, chaparral, woodlands.
Comments: Seeds are poisonous and flower nectar is believed to kill bees.

HEATHS
Family of trees, shrubs and flowering plants that grow in acidic soils.

PACIFIC MADRONE
Arbutus menziesii
Size: To 100 ft. (30 m)
Description: Tree with smooth, red-brown branches and glossy, evergreen leaves. Clusters of white flowers bloom in spring and are succeeded by red-orange berries that often persist into winter.
Habitat: Moist and rocky soils, mixed woodlands.
Comments: The reddish outer bark regularly peels off in thin sections, exposing the smooth green inner bark that gradually darkens with age.

COMMON MANZANITA
Arctostaphylos manzanita

Size: 10-20 ft. (3-6 m)
Description: Shrub or small tree with grotesquely twisted trunk(s) and branches. Bark is reddish and smooth; leaves are thick and finely-haired. Urn-shaped pink flowers bloom in early spring and are succeeded by small berry-like fruits.
Habitat: Chaparral, foothills, dry rocky slopes in northern California.
Comments: Berries are a valuable food source for wildlife. *Manzanita* is Spanish for 'small apples.'

COMPOSITES

This huge family of plants includes over 13,000 species worldwide.

COYOTE BRUSH
Baccharis pitularis

Size: 10-15 ft. (3-5 m)
Description: Wiry evergreen shrub or small branching tree. Coarsely toothed, dull gray-green leaves grow alternately. Whitish-green flowers bloom in tight clusters and are succeeded by 'hairy' seeds.
Habitat: Chaparral, foothills.
Comments: Very common in coastal scrub areas, often in association with blueblossom and poison oak.

PALMS, YUCCAS AND CACTI

These evergreens are common in the warmer regions of California. They differ from other trees by having leaves with parallel veins and trunks that lack growth rings. Most have been introduced from the tropics.

CALIFORNIA FAN PALM
Washingtonia filifera

Size: 20-60 ft. (6-18 m)
Description: Told at a glance by its crown of large, fan-shaped leaves and the shaggy sack of dead leaves hanging beneath it.
Habitat: Moist soils.
Comments: Native to southeast California, it has been widely introduced elsewhere.

DATE PALM
Phoenix dactylifera
Size: To 75 ft. (23 m)
Description: Distinguished by its stout trunk and crown of ascending palm leaves. Trunk is roughened by the vestiges of dead leaves. Large clusters of small yellow flowers are succeeded by pulpy fruits.
Habitat: Moist soils.
Comments: A common ornamental in warm regions.

CANARY PALM
Phoenix canariensis
Size: To 66 ft. (20 m)
Description: Tree with stout, straight trunk and enormous, feathery, evergreen leaves that grow to 23 ft. (7 m) long.
Habitat: Moist soils throughout southern California.
Comments: Introduced over a century ago, it is commonly planted along streets.

JOSHUA TREE
Yucca brevifolia
Size: 15-30 ft. (5-9 m)
Description: A many-branched tree with terminal tufts of short, stiff, dagger-like leaves 6-10 in. (15-25 cm) long. Clusters of yellow tubular flowers bloom March-May and are succeeded by oblong fruits 2-4 in. (5-10 cm) long.
Habitat: Dry soil on deserts, plains, hillsides.
Comments: Tree is a home for woodpeckers and fruit is a valuable source of food for desert wildlife.

COCONUT PALM
Cocos nucifera

Size: To 100 ft. (30 m)
Description: This classic desert-island palm is told by its smooth, often curved, trunk and large crown of feathery leaves. The familiar fruit is a fibrous nut 10-12 in. (25-30 cm) long.
Habitat: Most soils.
Comments: A widespread non-native species.

MOHAVE YUCCA
Yucca schidigera

Size. 10-20 ft. (3-6 m)
Description: Tree or shrub with upright branches and prominent, dagger-like leaves. White spring flower clusters are succeeded by cylindrical fruits.
Habitat: Found on dry soils at elevations to 5,000 ft. (1,500 m).
Comments: Indians obtained food, soap, blankets and ropes from this plant.

TEDDYBEAR CHOLLA
Opuntia bigelovii

Size: 3-9 ft. (.3-2.7 m)
Description: A small, fuzzy-looking tree with branches covered with numerous inch-long, barbed spines. Pink flowers bloom at branch tips in summer and are succeeded by green, pear-shaped fruits.
Habitat: Dry, open areas in deserts.
Comments: This cute-sounding plant is anything but cuddly; the sharp spines easily penetrate skin and are extremely difficult to remove.

WHAT ARE WILDFLOWERS?

Wildflowers are soft-stemmed flowering plants, smaller than trees or shrubs, that grow anew each year. Some regenerate annually from the same rootstock (perennials), while others grow from seeds and last a single season (annuals). Most have flowering stems bearing colorful blossoms which ripen into fruits as the growing season progresses. The flowering stem typically grows upright, but may be climbing, creeping or trailing. Wildflowers range from weeds and reeds to roses and buttercups and are found almost everywhere. From the cracks in sidewalks to mountain meadows, wildflowers are abundant and widespread throughout California.

N.B. – This section covers wildflowers and includes some shrubs that are conspicuous when in bloom.

The species in this section have been grouped according to color rather than family in order to facilitate field identification. The color groups used are:

- White
- Yellow, Orange and Green
- Red and Pink
- Blue and Purple

HOW TO IDENTIFY WILDFLOWERS

After noting color, examine the shape of the flower heads. Are they daisy-like, bell-shaped, or odd in appearance? How are they arranged on the plant? Do they occur singly or in clusters? Are the flower heads upright or drooping? Pay close attention to the leaves and how they are arranged on the stem. Refer to the illustrations and text to confirm its size, habitat and blooming period.

N.B. - The blooming periods of flowers can vary depending on latitude, elevation and the weather. The dates given are meant to serve as general guidelines only.

Remember that flowers are wildlife and should be treated as such. Many species have been seriously depleted due to loss of habitat and over-picking. In many areas, once-abundant species are now rare. Bring along a sketchbook and camera to record the flowers you see instead of picking them. This will help ensure there are more blossoms for you and others to enjoy next year.

FLOWER STRUCTURE

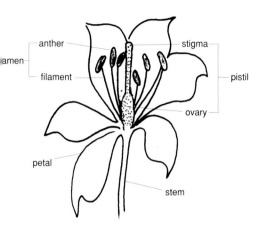

anther

stigma

amen

filament

pistil

petal

ovary

stem

FLOWER SHAPES

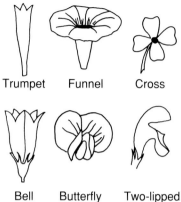

Trumpet   Funnel   Cross

Bell   Butterfly   Two-lipped

COMMON FRUITS

Drupe
junipers, cherries,
dogwoods, hollies

Acorn
oaks

Winged Seed
dandelions,
milkweeds,
poplars,
cottonwoods

Pod
peas,
mesquites,
locusts

Berry-like
blackberries,
oranges, tomatoes
-all have tiny
fruitlets joined
together to form a
larger fruit

Samara
maples, ashes,
hophornbeams,
elms

Pome
apples, plums,
yuccas, pears

Nut
chestnuts,
buckeyes,
walnuts, pecans,
hickories

WHITE FLOWERS

WHITE TRILLIUM
Trillium ovatum

Size: To 16 in. (40 cm)
Description: White, three-petalled flower is framed by a whorl of three broad leaves. Blooms February-June.
Habitat: Forest floors, stream banks in northern and central California.
Comments: Arrives with the robin in spring and is also referred to as western wake robin.

ENGLISH DAISY
Bellis perennis

Size: To 10 in. (25 cm)
Description: Slender, leafless stalk supports a single, yellow-centered white flower with numerous rays. Basal leaves are rounded. Blooms March-September.
Habitat: Fields, waste areas, roadsides.
Comments: A common lawn weed introduced from Europe.

WHITE VIRGIN'S-BOWER
Clematis ligusticifolia

Size: Vine
Description: Vine covered with numerous beautiful cream flowers. Opposite leaves have toothed leaflets and are up to 3 in. (8 cm) long. Blooms June-September.
Habitat: Canyons, gullies, chaparral, deserts.
Comments: Crushed leaves have a peppery aroma.

BINDWEED
Convolvulus arvensis

Size: To 3 ft. (90 cm)
Description: A twining plant
with beautiful, white to pinkish
funnel-shaped flowers. Blooms
May-October.
Habitat: Gardens, waste areas,
fields, farmlands.
Comments: Regarded as a weed by
many, it is very difficult to eradicate
because of its deep roots. A member
of the morning-glory family.

ELEGANT CAMAS
Zygadenus elegans

Size: To 28 in. (72 cm)
Description: Told by grass-like leaves
and branching cluster of white, lily-
like flowers that bloom during
summer months.
Habitat: Grassy slopes, mountain
meadows, open forests.
Comments: Its bulb and leaves are
very poisonous and can induce coma
in humans and livestock.

COMMON ICE PLANT
Mesembryanthemum crystallinum

Size: To 8 in. (20 cm)
Description: A creeping plant with
beaded, glistening stems. Showy
white or pinkish flowers bloom
April-October.
Habitat: Sandy soils in coastal
and desert regions in California.
Comments: The flowers open fully
only in direct sunlight.

COW PARSNIP
Heracleum lanatum

Size: To 10 ft. (3 m)
Description: A large, conspicuous plant. Deeply-lobed leaves grow along the length of its thick, hollow stem. Dense, flattened clusters of creamy white flowers bloom February-September, depending on location.
Habitat: Very common in moist fields and woods.
Comments: Though non-poisonous, it resembles similar plants, like the water hemlock, which are deadly.

WHITE SWEET CLOVER
Melilotus alba

Size: 2-7 ft. (.5-2.1 m)
Description: Tall leafy plant with long spikes of tiny, white, pea-shaped flowers. Blooms May-October.
Habitat: Roadsides, waste areas, fields.
Comments: Very common. Flowers have the scent of hay.

WHITE CLOVER
Trifolium repens

Size: To 12 in. (30 cm)
Description: Long-stemmed, dark green leaves have three oval leaflets and grow densely along creeping, mat-forming stems. Rounded white flowers bloom April-September.
Habitat: Common in fields, lawns and waste areas.
Comments: An excellent nectar producer, it is a favorite of bees. Red and pink clovers are also found in California.

PACIFIC DOGWOOD
Cornus nuttallii

Size: To 65 ft. (20 m)
Description: Typically a shrub or
small tree bearing numerous large
white or pinkish flowers. Small
greenish flowers grow within
the showy petal-like bracts.
Blooms April-June. Flowers
are succeeded by red berries
in fall.
Habitat: Undergrowth of dense
forests to 6,000 ft. (1,800 m).
Comments: Dogwoods are widely
planted as ornamentals and are
prized for their hard wood.

ARROWHEAD
Sagittaria latifolia

Size: To 3 ft. (90 cm)
Description: Small, white lily-like
flowers bloom above arrow-shaped
leaves during summer months.
Habitat: Ponds, slow streams,
marshes, ditches.
Comments: The plant produces
underground tubers that were
an important food source for
early settlers.

OUR LORD'S CANDLE
Yucca whipplei

Size: To 10 ft. (3 m)
Description: Stout, spiny stalk
supports huge, elongate cluster of
cream to white, bell-shaped flowers.
Blooms March-May.
Habitat: Chaparral.
Comments: Often blooms by the
hundreds on brushy slopes in
southern California.

YARROW
Achillea millefolium

Size: To 2 ft. (60 cm)
Description: A long, unbranched stem supports dense clusters of round, yellow-centered daisy-like flowers. Each flower has four to six white (occasionally pinkish) rays. The unusual fern-like leaves are a good field mark. Blooms March-October.
Habitat: Common in ditches, fields and waste areas.
Comments: An aromatic herb, it is also known as milfoil.

PHLOX
Phlox spp.

Size: To 18 in. (45 cm)
Description: Sprawling herbs or small shrubs with numerous showy, five-lobed, yellow-centered flowers. Petals fold back from a narrow tube. Flowers range in color from pink and lavender to yellow and white, and several variants may be found within a small area. Blooms April-September.
Habitat: Dry soils in a variety of habitats.
Comments: About 12 species of phlox are found in California.

POISON OAK
Toxicodendron diversilobum

Size: To 13 ft. (4 m)
Description: An upright shrub or climbing vine with drooping leaves and white berries in loose clusters along the stem. Leaves have three rounded or oak-like leaflets. Small whitish flowers bloom in summer and are succeeded by hard, whitish berries. Plant is showy in fall when its leaves turn bright red.
Habitat: Shaded woods, chaparral, brushy slopes.
Comments: Contact with the leaves, stems or flowers can cause a severe rash. Washing affected area thoroughly with soap and water is recommended.

BEACH STRAWBERRY
Fragaria chiloensis

Size: To 8 in. (20 cm)
Description: Mat-forming plant has coarsely-toothed, leathery leaves with three leaflets. Crisp white flowers bloom March-August and are succeeded in late summer by the familiar fruit.
Habitat: Open areas, forest margins, hillsides.
Comments: This plant commonly interbreeds with the domestic strawberry.

DESERT LILY
Hesperocallis undulata

Size: To 5 ft. (1.5 m)
Description: Large, funnel-shaped white flowers are unmistakable. Narrow leaves have wavy edges. Blooms March-May.
Habitat: Sandy soils in southeastern California.
Comments: Easily spotted when driving through the desert region.

YELLOW, ORANGE AND GREEN FLOWERS

CALIFORNIA POPPY
Eschscholzia californica

Size: To 2 ft. (60 cm)
Description: Distinguished by its delicate yellow-orange flowers and fern-like leaves. Blooms February-September.
Habitat: Open areas.
Comments: The flowers are light sensitive and close at night. Common throughout California, it is the state flower.

SUBALPINE BUTTERCUP
Ranunculus eschscholtzii

Size: To 10 in. (25 cm)
Description: Shiny, yellow flower with five overlapping petals and smooth, oval leaves. Blooms June-August.
Habitat: Mountain meadows, rocky slopes, fields.
Comments: One of over 20 species of buttercup found in California.

DESERT CANDLE
Caulanthus inflatus

Size: To 2 ft. (60 cm)
Description: Slender yellow-stemmed plant covered in small white or purplish flower. Blooms May-July.
Habitat: Deserts, dry slopes. Often associated with sagebrush.
Comments: Related to mustard plants.

GOLDFIELDS
Lasthenia chrysostoma

Size: To 10 in. (25 cm)
Description: Slender, reddish stems with opposite, narrow leaves support small yellow flowers. Blooms in spring.
Habitat: Poor soils, open, dry areas.
Comments: When enough moisture is available, this flower literally blankets open areas with gold.

COMMON SUNFLOWER
Helianthus annuus

Size: To 10 ft. (3 m)
Description: Tall, leafy plant with a branching stem supporting numerous yellow, dark-centered flowers. Blooms June-September.
Habitat: Roadsides, waste areas, open fields.
Comments: Flowers follow the sun across the sky each day.

GOLDENROD
Solidago canadensis

Size: To 5 ft. (1.5 m)
Description: Tall, leafy plant with spreading, arched clusters of tiny yellow flowers. Leaves are hairy with three distinct veins. Blooms May-September.
Habitat: Meadows, pastures, open forests.
Comments: Widespread to the point that it is considered a nuisance in some areas.

BLAZING STAR
Mentzelia laevicaulis

Size: To 3 ft. (90 cm)
Description: Large, star-shaped, waxy yellow flowers feature a central puff of long stamens. Flowers bloom at the tips of white, satiny stems between June-September.
Habitat: Waste areas, roadsides, deserts.
Comments: A member of the stick-tight family, it has toothed leaves covered with barbed hairs that cling to fabric.

WOOLLY MULLEIN
Verbascum thapsus

Size: To 6 ft. (1.8 m)
Description: Tall leafy plant that tapers from a broad base to a slender spike of yellow flowers. Flowers bloom a few at a time throughout summer.
Habitat: Roadsides, fields and waste areas.
Comments: Gold miners used to make torches from these plants by dipping them in tallow.

COMMON DANDELION
Taraxacum officinale

Size: To 12 in. (30 cm)
Description: Told by its elongate, toothed leaves and shaggy yellow flowers that bloom frequently throughout the growing season. Tufts of whitish, hairy seeds succeed the flowers and are dispersed by the wind.
Habitat: Abundant in open and grassy areas.
Comments: The leaves are often used in salads and the blossoms for wine-making.

KLAMATH WEED
Hypericum perforatum

Size: To 5 ft. (1.5 m)
Description: Branching, leafy stem supports a cluster of star-shaped yellow flowers, often with black dots near the tips. Blooms June-September.
Habitat: Pastures, roadsides and waste areas.
Comments: A troublesome weed very common throughout California. Can be poisonous to livestock.

SHRUBBY CINQUEFOIL
Potentilla fruticosa

Size: To 3 ft. (90 cm)
Description: Small, woody plant with reddish, shredding bark and yellow flowers. Toothed leaves have three or five lobes. Blooms June-August.
Habitat: Pastures, roadsides, hillsides, gardens, meadows.
Comments: Widely cultivated as an ornamental.

YELLOW VIOLET
Viola glabella

Size: To 12 in. (30 cm)
Description: Yellow flower has conspicuous dark veins on three of its five petals. Heart-shaped leaves have sharply pointed tips.
Habitat: Very common in moist forests, clearings and near streams at low to middle elevations.
Comments: Several other species of mauve, blue and white violets are found in California.

HOOKER'S EVENING PRIMROSE
Oenothera hookeri

Size: To 3 ft. (1 m)
Description: Tall plant with long, slender leaves. Large, four-petalled yellow flowers bloom June-September.
Habitat: Roadsides and grassy slopes from low to middle elevations.
Comments: As the common name suggests, the flowers open near the end of the day.

COMMON MONKEY FLOWER
Mimulus guttatus

Size: To 5 ft. (1.5 m)
Description: Trumpet-shaped yellow flowers have dark-spotted, hairy throats. Oval leaves are coarsely toothed; lower leaves are stalked, upper ones are clasping. Flowers bloom in loose terminal clusters March-September.
Habitat: Wet areas, meadows, and ditches at most elevations.
Comments: Pink, purple, red and white monkey flowers are also found in California.

CREAMCUPS
Platystemon californicus

Size: To 12 in. (30 cm)
Description: Hairy plant with narrow, opposite leaves. Bowl-shaped, six-petalled yellow flowers bloom atop slender stalks March-May.
Habitat: Moist meadows, fields, hillsides.
Comments: Grows in dense colonies and often covers entire fields.

RABBITBRUSH
Chrysothamnus nauseosus

Size: 3-7 ft. (.9-2.1 m)
Description: Small shrub with wiry, hairy stems. Terminal clusters of small yellow flowers bloom August-October.
Habitat: Grasslands and dry areas mainly in the Great Basin region.
Comments: An important food source for jackrabbits and deer.

TARWEED
Madia elegans

Size: To 4 ft. (1.2 m)
Description: Stem is hairy and sticky; leaves are long and narrow. Flower petals (rays) are toothed near the outer edge and maroon-colored near the base.
Habitat: Dry areas, along roadsides.
Comments: Named for its sticky stem, it is abundant throughout California. Also called common madia.

BARREL CACTUS
Ferocactus acanthodes

Size: 3-10 ft. (1-3 m)
Description: Yellowish flowers bloom atop this rounded cactus in spring.
Habitat: Dry hills, gravelly slopes.
Comments: Its succulent stem is able to absorb large amounts of water during short rainy spells. Spines help to reduce water loss by evaporation.

GREAT BASIN SAGEBRUSH
Artemisia tridentata

Size: To 2-20 ft. (.6-6 m)
Description: Gray-green shrub or small tree with narrow, three-toothed, wedge-shaped leaves. Inconspicuous yellowish flowers bloom at stem tips.
Habitat: Deserts, mountain slopes and plains in eastern California.
Comments: Plant emits an aromatic 'sage' odor when handled. Important food source for deer, grouse and livestock. Coastal sagebrush (*Artemisia californica*), common along the southwest coast of California, has thin, grass-like leaves.

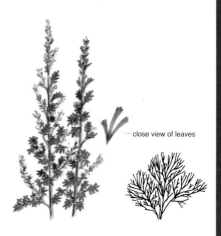

close view of leaves

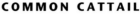

COMMON CATTAIL
Typha latifolia

Size: To 10 ft. (3 m)
Description: Distinguished by its prominent club-like sheath of greenish flower spikes atop a long stalk. The flowers ripen into brownish tufts of hairy seeds in late summer.
Habitat: Common in marshes, ditches and along lakes and rivers.
Comments: Cattails provide a vital source of food and cover for water birds and wildlife.

STINGING NETTLE
Urtica gracilis

Size: To 10 ft. (3 m)
Description: Coarsely saw-toothed, opposite leaves have sharp prickles that eject an acidic stinging fluid (formic acid) on contact. Drooping spikes of green flowers bloom June-August.
Habitat: Shady thickets, meadows, waste areas, along creeks.
Comments: Common throughout California.

COMMON PLANTAIN
Plantago major

Size: To 20 in. (50 cm)
Description: Large, tough basal leaves are finely-toothed with deep longitudinal veins. Tiny greenish flowers bloom in a slender spike.
Habitat: Very common in lawns, gardens and waste areas.
Comments: An introduced weed widespread throughout the country.

RED AND PINK FLOWERS

SKYROCKET
Ipomopsis aggregata

Size: To 7 ft. (2.1 m)
Description: Slender stems support clusters of bright red, tubular flowers resembling exploded fireworks. Blooms May-September.
Habitat: Open woodlands, dry hillsides.
Comments: Foliage has a skunky odor.

FIREWEED
Epilobium angustifolium

Size: To 7 ft. (2 m)
Description: Distinguished by a long conical spike of bright pink, four-petalled flowers. Blooms June-September.
Habitat: Very common in open woodlands, clearings and burned-out areas.
Comments: Often grows in dense colonies.

INDIAN PAINTBRUSH
Castilleja spp.

Size: To 3 ft. (90 cm)
Description: Ragged red wildflower often grows in dense colonies. Blooms May-September.
Habitat: Woodlands and mountain meadows.
Comments: Related to snapdragons, paintbrushes occur in a variety of colors. Many are parasitic on other plants. 33 species occur in California.

BEAVERTAIL CACTUS
Opuntia basilaris

Size: To 10 ft. (3 m)
Description: Jointed, flattened cactus segments grow in clumps. Showy pink flowers bloom April-June.
Habitat: Deserts, rocky slopes.
Comments: Widely planted as an ornamental in southern California.

FAREWELL-TO-SPRING
Clarkia amoena

Size: To 3 ft. (90 cm)
Description: Slender, branching stem with showy, pinkish, poppy-like flowers. Petals often have a central blotch of maroon. Blooms June-August.
Habitat: Open woods and grassy slopes in coastal northern California.
Comments: Flowers close at night and re-open in the morning.

FRINGE CUPS
Tellima grandiflora

Size: To 30 in. (76 cm)
Description: Pinkish to white, cup-shaped, fringed flowers grow along slender stalks rising from a leafy base. Blooms May-July.
Habitat: Moist, shaded woodlands in northern California.
Comments: Abundant along the coast.

REDWOOD SORREL
Oxalis oregana

Size: To 6 in. (15 cm)
Description: Tiny pink flowers bloom amidst a carpet of shamrock-shaped leaves from April-September. Leaflets often have a pale blotch down their middle.
Habitat: Moist, shaded woods.
Comments: Abundant in the understorey of redwood forests.

CREEPING THISTLE
Cirsium arvense

Size: To 5 ft. (1.5 m)
Description: Tall plant with scalloped, prickly leaves and puffy pink flowers. Blooms May-October.
Habitat: Fields, ditches, waste areas.
Comments: This ubiquitous weed is common throughout North America, Asia and Europe. Flowers are sweet-smelling and rich in nectar.

WOODS' ROSE
Rosa woodsii

Size: To 5 ft. (1.5 m)
Description: A prickly shrub with broad, pink, five-petalled, sweet-smelling flowers. Blooms April-September.
Habitat: Open areas and woodlands.
Comments: Flowers are succeeded by fruits called 'hips' that are rich in vitamin C and used in teas. At least eight other species of wild roses occur in California.

FOXGLOVE
Digitalis purpurea

Size: To 7 ft. (2 m)
Description: Showy plant with prominent cluster of nodding lavender flowers. Blooms June-July.
Habitat: Disturbed areas, wooded slopes, roadsides. Especially abundant near coast.
Comments: An extract from this plant is the heart stimulant, digitalis.

CALIFORNIA RHODODENDRON
Rhododendron macrophyllum

Size: To 25 ft. (7.6 m)
Description: Handsome flowering shrub or small tree with broad clusters of white to pink, trumpet-shaped flowers. Large, leathery evergreen leaves have edges rolled under. Blooms April-August.
Habitat: Moist, shaded areas in forests below 4,000 ft. (1,220 m).
Comments: Associated with pines, redwoods and Douglas-fir.

CARDINAL FLOWER
Lobelia cardinalis

Size: To 3 ft. (90 cm)
Description: Plant with spike of striking, red tubular flowers. Blooms June-October.
Habitat: Wet, open areas, moist woods in southern California.
Comments: Also called scarlet lobelia, its flowers are a favorite of hummingbirds.

RED COLUMBINE
Aquilegia formosa

Size: To 3 ft. (90 cm)
Description: Stunning red-orange flower head with tall spurs is unmistakable. Blooms May-August.
Habitat: Open woods, meadows, glades.
Comments: Blue and white columbines are also found in California.

SHOOTING STAR
Dodecatheon pulchellum

Size: To 20 in. (50 cm)
Description: Graceful plant with drooping, dart-like reddish flowers with inverted petals exposing yellow stamen tube. Blooms May-August.
Habitat: Moist soils in meadows, fields and open woodlands.
Comments: Several similar species are found in California. Related to primroses and cyclamens.

PINE DROPS
Pterospora andromedea

Size: To 3 ft. (90 cm)
Description: Slender, hairy, red-brown stalks covered with small, yellowish egg-shaped flowers.
Habitat: Coniferous forests.
Comments: Is a root parasite of conifers. Commonly associated with ponderosa pine.

DESERT GLOBEMALLOW
Sphaeralcea ambigua
Size: To 40 in. (1 m)
Description: Hairy, branching plant with striking red-orange flowers. Leaves are three-lobed and coarsely toothed. Blooms March-June.
Habitat: Deserts.
Comments: Genus name refers to the spherical fruit that succeeds the flowers.

CALIFORNIA FUCHSIA
Zauschneria californica
Size: To 3 ft. (90 cm)
Description: Bushy, gray-green plant with a profusion of red, tubular flowers. Blooms August-October.
Habitat: Dry slopes from sea level to upper mountain elevations.
Comments: This late-bloomer is easily spotted in autumn. Is an important food source for hummingbirds.

BITTERROOT
Lewisia rediviva
Size: To 2 in. (5 cm)
Description: Ground-hugging plant with beautiful pinkish flowers. Blooms March-June.
Habitat: Barren, dry ground, gravelly slopes and rocky areas.
Comments: Associated with sagebrush and pines. Also called sandrose.

STRIPED CORAL ROOT
Corallorhiza striata

Size: To 20 in. (50 cm)
Description: Medium-sized plant with a spire of dark-striped flowers.
Habitat: Moist woodlands.
Comments: Lacks chlorophyll and obtains food by absorbing nutrients from the organic matter it grows on.

PIPSISSEWA
Chimaphila umbellata

Size: To 10 in. (25 cm)
Description: Leathery, evergreen leaves are coarsely-toothed and whorled around the stem. Small, saucer-shaped, waxy pink flowers bloom in nodding clusters of 3-10 between June-August.
Habitat: Found in cool, moist coniferous forests.
Comments: Leaves were once used as a tea substitute by early settlers.

BLUE AND PURPLE FLOWERS

ELEGANT BRODIAEA
Brodiaea elegans

Size: To 16 in. (40 cm)
Description: Leafless stalk supports several funnel-shaped, blue-purple flowers that bloom April-July.
Habitat: Dry soils, grasslands.
Comments: 37 species of brodiaea are found in the western states.

SHOWY MILKWEED
Ascelpias speciosa

Size: To 4 ft. (1.2 m)

Description: Red-purplish, horned flowers bloom in tight clusters May-August. Large, fleshy leaves are finely-haired. In autumn, long seed pods split open to release thousands of conspicuous, long-plumed seeds.

Habitat: Dry soils in waste areas and ditches, open forests.

Comments: Both the leaves and stem secrete a sticky fluid to protect the flowers from crawling insects.

BABY BLUE EYES
Nemophila menziesii

Size: To 12 in. (30 cm)

Description: Low, mat-forming plant with pale blue, five-petalled flowers. Petals are typically paler near the base and spotted with black dots. Blooms February-June.

Habitat: Open woods, meadows.

Comments: A well-known, popular wildflower that is sold commercially.

COMMON CAMAS
Camassia quamash

Size: To 24 in. (60 cm)

Description: Striking blue, star-shaped flowers bloom April-June. Leaves are narrow and grass-like.

Habitat: Moist soils in meadows and open areas.

Comments: Often cover entire meadows. Plant bulbs were food for native Indians.

CHICORY
Cichorium intybus

Size: To 6 ft. (1.8 m)
Description: Wheel-shaped, pale blue flowers bloom atop slender branching stems April-October.
Habitat: Fields, roadsides, waste areas.
Comments: The roots are used as a coffee substitute.

FRINGED GENTIAN
Gentiana detonsa

Size: To 15 in. (38 cm)
Description: Beautiful blue-violet, bell-shaped flowers have delicately fringed edges. Blooms in summer.
Habitat: Moist areas in the foothills and mountains.
Comments: Often cultivated as an ornamental.

MINIATURE LUPINE
Lupinus bicolor

Size: To 14 in. (36 cm)
Description: Branching, hairy plant with bluish flowers arranged in whorls around the stem. Blooms March-May.
Habitat: Open slopes, grassy areas,
Comments: Often associated with the California poppy, it grows in dense colonies and may blanket entire fields.

SALSIFY
Tragopogon porrifolius
Size: To 4 ft. (1.2 m)
Description: Purple flower head blooms atop a swollen stem during summer.
Habitat: Fields, waste areas.
Comments: Also called oyster plant, its root has the flavor of oysters when cooked.

WILD BLUE FLAX
Linum perenne
Size: To 30 in. (76 cm)
Description: Delicate sky-blue, yellow-centered flowers bloom atop slender, wiry stems March-September.
Habitat: Prairies, meadows, hillsides.
Comments: The tough stems were used by native Indians to make cords.

AMERICAN VETCH
Vicia americana
Size: To 4 ft. long (1.2 m)
Description: A climbing vine with clusters of 4-10 purplish, pea-shaped flowers. Flowers turn blue as they age. Blooms April-July.
Habitat: Open woodlands, roadsides.
Comments: Similar to a number of wild pea plants.

MISSION BELLS
Fritillaria lanceolata

Size: To 40 in. (1 m)
Description: Dark purple-brown, nodding, bell-shaped flowers with bright yellow anthers. Narrow leaves grow in whorls around the stem.
Habitat: Open woods, grassy areas.
Comments: Named by the early Spanish priests who founded the first missions

TEASEL
Dipsacus sylvestris

Size: To 7 ft. (2.1 m)
Description: Prickly plant with a spikey purple flower head. Grass-like, erect leaves are also prickly on their undersides. Blooms April-September.
Habitat: Moist soils, fields, open woodlands.
Comments: Related to the garden variety pincushions.

BLUE-EYED GRASS
Sisyrinchium angustifolium

Size: To 2 ft. (60 cm)
Description: Slender stems support one or more delicate, 6-petalled, star-shaped blue-violet flowers. Blooms March-September.
Habitat: Moist areas in woodlands and meadows.
Comments: Its yellow cousin, golden-eyed grass, is also found in California.

CALIFORNIA REGIONS

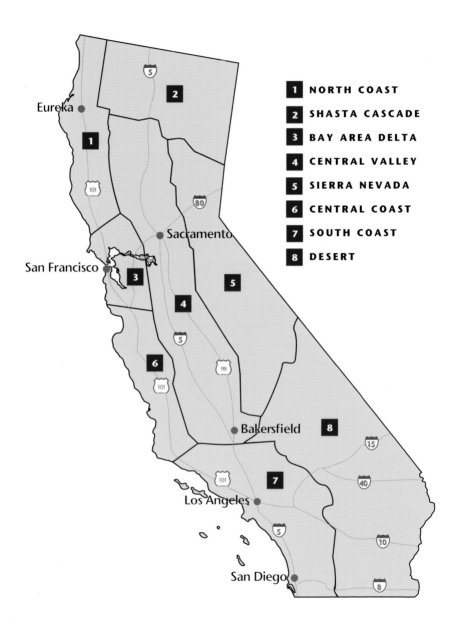

1 NORTH COAST
2 SHASTA CASCADE
3 BAY AREA DELTA
4 CENTRAL VALLEY
5 SIERRA NEVADA
6 CENTRAL COAST
7 SOUTH COAST
8 DESERT

Californians have dedicated hundreds of parks, sanctuaries and museums to preserve and showcase the state's natural beauty. This precious heritage provides unsurpassed educational and recreational benefits for residents and tourists alike.

We have divided California into eight regions that generally reflect the biodiversity in different parts of the state.

1 NORTH COAST

Stretching for over 300 miles, the North Coast is characterized by primeval forests of towering redwoods and a rugged, often fog-shrouded coast. This land's raw beauty appeals to nature lovers and casual travellers who come to explore old growth forests, magnificent shorelines, coastal tidepools and seek out herds of grazing elk.

2 SHASTA CASCADE

This region is less commercialized than most of California and offers visitors some of the best back-country adventuring the state has to offer. The scenery in the north is dominated by Mount Shasta, a huge, dormant volcano visible for over 100 miles. The Lassen Volcanic National Park provides visitors with a glimpse of current volcanic activity in its hot pools and bubbling mudpots.

3 BAY AREA DELTA

A richly endowed region, the Bay Area Delta is known for its vast tidal marshes, rich farmland and prominent sanctuaries and museums. The region's expansive wetlands attract an abundance of migrating birds and serve as a vital nursery for fish fry and shellfish.

4 CENTRAL VALLEY

This region is a major off-ramp of the Pacific flyway, an aerial highway used by millions of birds during migrations. While the majority of birds merely stop to refuel, many stay to nest. This region is also the most productive farming area in the state and has thousands of miles of waterways.

5 SIERRA NEVADA

The Sierra Nevada Mountains are home to some of California's greatest natural treasures. Giant sequoias, the largest living trees, grace several state and national parks. Lake Tahoe is one of the largest and deepest alpine lakes on earth. Yosemite's breathtaking waterfalls and pristine wilderness attract millions of visitors each year from around the world.

6 CENTRAL COAST

This region encompasses what many believe to be the most spectacular coastal area of California. Major attractions include battling bull elephant seals, 'Butterfly Town U.S.A.,' the world-renowned Monterey Bay Aquarium and the extensive coastal dune systems in the south.

7 SOUTH COAST

It is not surprising that this heavily-populated region is most famous for its man-made sanctuaries and museums. Sea World, the San Diego Zoo, the Museum of La Brea Discoveries and the San Diego Wild Animal Park are all top attractions. For the adventurous, a trip to the remote Channel Islands sanctuary provides excellent wildlife viewing opportunities.

8 DESERT

The expansive desert region is home to a variety of unusual plants and animals adapted to the hot, dry climate. Though home to the hottest place in the western hemisphere – Death Valley – California's deserts also feature a number of lush habitats that harbor a diversity of wildlife.

NORTH COAST

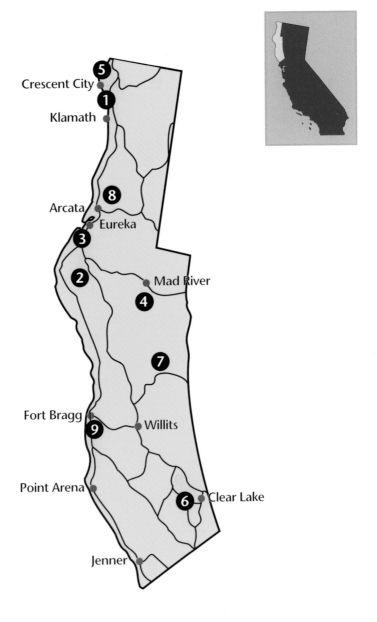

Crescent City

Klamath

Arcata

Eureka

Mad River

Fort Bragg

Willits

Point Arena

Clear Lake

Jenner

Parks/Wildlife Areas

❶ REDWOOD NATIONAL PARK

This 110,000-acre park features vast groves of coastal redwoods (including the world's tallest trees), salt marshes, sandy beaches, rivers and lakes and about 30 miles of coastline. Reservations required for campgrounds May-September. Stop at Redwood Information Centre in Orick to get a free permit to drive to the redwood grove featuring the world's first-, third- and fifth-tallest trees.
Location: Crescent City
Phone: (707) 464-6101

❷ HUMBOLDT REDWOODS STATE PARK

The famous Avenue of the Giants – an unforgettable 33-mile drive through some of the tallest trees on earth – traverses the length of this 51,000-acre park. Features include Founder's Grove and the 10,000-acre Rockefeller Forest. Numerous parking areas, picnic sites and nature trails.
Location: South of Eureka
Phone: (707) 946-2409

❸ HUMBOLDT BAY NATIONAL WILDLIFE REFUGE

Huge eelgrass beds, tidal flats, mudflats and grasslands. Major staging area for black brant geese (up to 40,000 at a time) in spring and fall.
Location: South of Eureka
Phone: (707) 733-5406

❹ RUTH LAKE

Bald eagles, herons, deer and otters are just a few of the resident species at this out-of-the-way refuge. Considered a birding hotspot, it is one of the region's best kept secrets.
Location: South of Mad River
Phone: (707) 524-6233

❺ LAKE EARL WILDLIFE AREA

Fresh- and saltwater marshes surrounded by groves of alder and spruce provide staging areas for 100,000 migratory waterfowl.
Location: North of Crescent City
Phone: (707) 464-2523

❻ CLEAR LAKE STATE PARK

California's second-largest freshwater lake is a popular resort and fishing area. Spring wildflower displays and fall colors are two annual highlights. Excellent birding year round with up to half a million wintering birds.
Location: Near Clear Lake
Phone: (707) 279-4293

❼ MENDOCINO NATIONAL FOREST

More than 1,000,000 acres of mountainous and rolling terrain along California's north coast.
Location: Northeast of Willits
Phone: (916) 934-3316

Museums/Sanctuaries

❽ HUMBOLDT STATE UNIVERSITY NATURAL HISTORY MUSEUM

Exhibits of over 2,000 species of ancient and living plants and animals. Collection of fossils includes saber-toothed cats, a *Tyrannosaurus rex* skull and jaws of 70-foot great white shark.
Location: Arcata
Phone: (707) 826-4479

❾ MENDOCINO COAST BOTANICAL GARDEN

Nature trails and two miles of coastal trails wind through 47 acres of gardens, woods and meadows.
Location: Near Fort Bragg
Phone: (707) 964-4352

SHASTA CASCADE

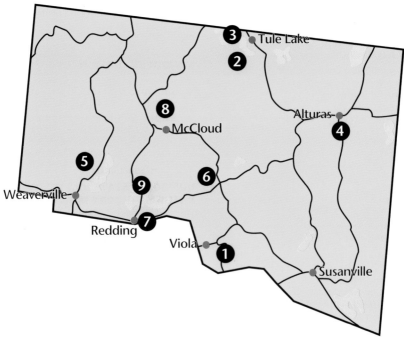

Parks/Wildlife Areas

❶ LASSEN VOLCANIC NATIONAL PARK

Features 100,000 acres of alpine wilderness and over 50 lakes. Mt. Lassen, the world's largest plug volcano, was active earlier this century, erupting 300 times between 1914-1922. Attractions include boiling lakes, bubbling mud pools, fumaroles and sulphur vents. Paths wind around and over some fascinating thermal areas.

Location: East of Viola
Phone: (916) 595-4444

❷ LAVA BEDS NATIONAL MONUMENT

Lava tube caves, cinder cones and lava flows are just a few of the attractions that can be explored at this dormant volcano.

Location: Tule Lake
Phone: (916) 667-2282

❸ KLAMATH BASIN NATIONAL WILDLIFE REFUGES

Six refuges of 86,000 acres encompass a variety of habitats including wetlands, marshes, farmlands and uplands. Fall migrations bring up to two million birds, primarily geese and ducks. Bald eagles are a common winter visitor.

Location: Near Tule Lake
Phone: (916) 667-2231

❹ MODOC NATIONAL WILDLIFE REFUGE

A 6,200 acre refuge with numerous lakes, ponds, streams, marshes and farmland.

Location: Alturas
Phone: (916) 233-3572

❺ SHASTA-TRINITY NATIONAL FOREST

2.1 million-acre forest features high mountains (Mt. Shasta 14,161 ft.), rolling hills, river valleys, 131 lakes and numerous rivers and streams. Contains California's second largest wilderness area.

Location: Weaverville
Phone: (916) 246-5222

❻ McARTHUR-BURNEY FALLS MEMORIAL STATE PARK

Highlight is a 129-ft. waterfall that Teddy Roosevelt called the eighth wonder of the world. 100 million gallons of water rush over the falls each day.

Location: Northeast of Redding
Phone: (916) 335-2777

Museums/Sanctuaries

❼ CARTER HOUSE NATURAL SCIENCE MUSEUM

Features exhibits on local natural history and science.

Location: Redding
Phone: (916) 243-5457

❽ MOUNT SHASTA FISH HATCHERY

The oldest fish hatchery in western North America features pools with over 100,000 trout. Trout viewing and feeding.

Location: Mt. Shasta
Phone: (916) 926-2215

❾ LAKE SHASTA CAVERNS

Lake Shasta boasts 370 miles of shoreline and a series of spectacular caverns where visitors can view stalactites, stalagmites and raw crystal formations.

Location: Lake Shasta
Phone: (916) 238-2341

BAY AREA DELTA

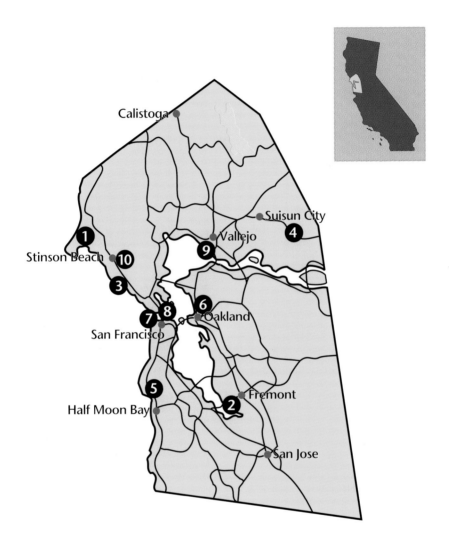

Calistoga

Suisun City

Vallejo

1

Stinson Beach **10**

9

4

3

8

6

7

Oakland

San Francisco

5

Fremont

Half Moon Bay

2

San Jose

Parks/Wildlife Areas

❶ POINT REYES NATIONAL SEASHORE

Meadows, bays, streams, lagoons, beaches and more than 800 flowering plants make this 73,000-acre sanctuary an exceptional birding area. Point Reyes Bird Sanctuary is located within the National Seashore.
Location: Point Reyes Station
Phone: (415) 663-1092

❷ SAN FRANCISCO BAY NATIONAL WILDLIFE REFUGE

20,000 acres of grassy uplands, mudflats, marshlands and tidal flats support a diversity of bird life.
Location: Near Fremont
Phone: (510) 792-0222

❸ MUIR WOODS NATIONAL MONUMENT

One of the most majestic and accessible redwood groves has trees up to 250 ft. tall (76 m) and over 1,000 years old.
Location: North of San Francisco
Phone: (415) 388-2595

❹ GRIZZLY ISLAND WILDLIFE AREA

The largest estuarine marsh in the U.S. provides excellent birding and nature study opportunities.
Location: Near Suisun City
Phone: (707) 425-3828

❺ FITZGERALD MARINE RESERVE

Observe all varieties of seashore life up close in California's largest natural tidal pools.
Location: Half Moon Bay
Phone: (415) 728-3584

Museums/Sanctuaries

❻ OAKLAND MUSEUM

A complex of galleries and gardens feature dramatic exhibits on native plants and animals that provide an excellent introduction to the natural history of California.
Location: Oakland
Phone: (510) 834-2413

❼ CALIFORNIA ACADEMY OF SCIENCES

The oldest science institution in the western U.S. is a museum, aquarium and planetarium rolled into one. Innovative exhibits highlight native wildlife and plants, evolution, human cultures and astronomy.
Location: San Francisco
Phone: (415) 750-7145

❽ STRYBING ARBORETUM AND BOTANICAL GARDEN

More than 5,000 species of plants on 70 acres. Features fragrance garden, Mediterranean collection, and moonviewing pavilion.
Location: San Francisco
Phone: (415) 661-1316

❾ MARINE WORLD AFRICA/USA

Famous oceanarium and 160-acre wildlife park has over 1,000 animals. Highlights include themed shows, ecology theater, butterfly world, petting zoo, and elephant and camel rides. Ferry service is available from San Francisco.
Location: Vallejo
Phone: (707) 643-6722

❿ AUDUBON CANYON RANCH

Numerous trails wind through this 1,000-acre sanctuary encompassing redwood groves and a salt marsh. Features heron and egret nesting sites, a museum and bookstore.
Location: Stinson Beach
Phone: (415) 868-9244

CENTRAL VALLEY

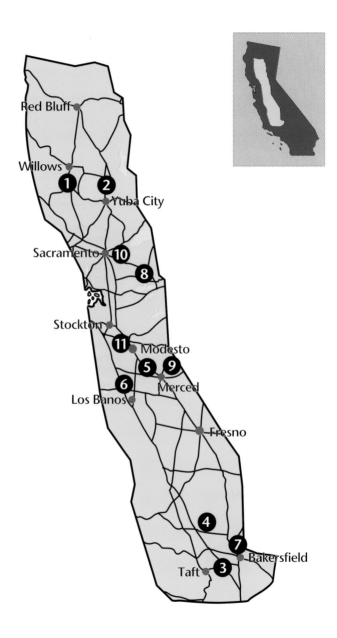

Parks/Wildlife Areas

❶ SACRAMENTO NATIONAL WILDLIFE REFUGE

The single most important refuge on the Pacific flyway attracts over two million migrating ducks and geese. Man-made marshes are intensely managed to provide an ideal wetland habitat. A birder's paradise throughout the year.
Location: Near Willows
Phone: (916) 934-2801

❷ GRAY LODGE WILDLIFE AREA

Over 6,500 acres of ponds attract more than 230 bird species and millions of migrating waterfowl. Bird populations peak October–January.
Location: North of Yuba City
Phone: (707) 425-3828

❸ TULE ELK STATE RESERVE

Reserve sustains four endangered species and herds of majestic tule elk. Marshes, ponds and grasslands support a wide diversity of plant and animal life. Guided tours are available.
Location: Near Bakersfield
Phone: (209) 822-2332

❹ KERN NATIONAL WILDLIFE REFUGE

Over 10,000 acres of marshes and grassland support an abundance of birds including waterfowl, shorebirds, herons and birds of prey.
Location: Delano
Phone: (805) 725-2767

❺ CASWELL MEMORIAL STATE PARK

Over 250 acres of virgin stands of huge oaks, willows and cottonwoods. Abundant birds and mammals.
Location: Near Modesto
Phone: (209) 599-3810

❻ LOS BANOS WILDLIFE AREA

3,200-acre grassland/wetland ecosystem supports a vast array of wildlife including over 200 species of birds. This is one of many wildlife refuges in the Central Valley that are carefully managed in order to divert large bird populations from surrounding farm crops.
Location: Los Banos
Phone: (209) 826-0463

Museums/Sanctuaries

❼ CALIFORNIA LIVING MUSEUM

Botanical garden and zoo feature native plants and animals.
Location: Bakersfield
Phone: (805) 872-2256

❽ MERCER CAVERNS

Since 1885 people have come to marvel at ancient crystalline and rock formations in 10 caverns. Guided tours.
Location: Murphys
Phone: (209) 728-2101

❾ YOSEMITE WILDLIFE MUSEUM

Features impressive dioramas of North American wildlife.
Location: Merced
Phone: (209) 383-1052

❿ NIMBUS HATCHERIES

Migrating chinook salmon and steelhead can be seen in autumn and winter climbing the fish ladder below Nimbus Dam. Hatchery raises over four million fry annually.
Location: Near Sacramento
Phone: (916) 355-0666

⓫ GREAT VALLEY MUSEUM OF NATURAL HISTORY

Highlights the natural history of the Central Valley and local plants and animals.
Location: Modesto
Phone: (209) 575-6196

SIERRA NEVADA

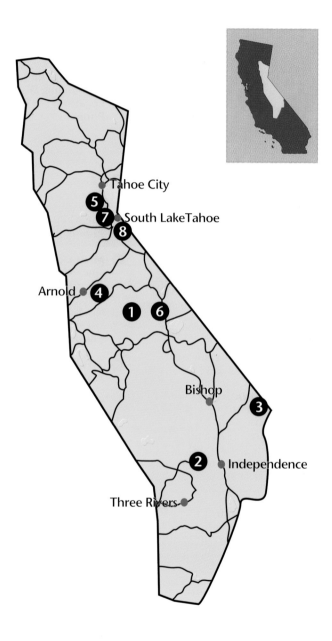

Tahoe City

South LakeTahoe

Arnold

Bishop

Independence

Three Rivers

Parks/Wildlife Areas

The Sierra National Parks are world-renowned for their spectacular scenery and natural attractions.

❶ YOSEMITE NATIONAL PARK

California's first national park is arguably its most famous natural attraction. Located in the heart of the Sierra Nevada, it features spectacular waterfalls, groves of giant sequoias, huge alpine meadows, pinnacles, canyons, lakes and rivers. Two of its waterfalls are among the 10 highest on earth. Three visitor centers, four museums, tours, guided hikes, extensive interpretive programs and hotel and campground accommodations are available.
Location: Yosemite National Park
Phone: (209) 372-0200

❷ SEQUOIA AND KINGS CANYON NATIONAL PARKS

Adjacent parks in the southern Sierra feature thousands of acres of giant sequoias in a breathtaking alpine setting. Among the sequoias are the two largest trees on earth (in mass). Highlights include Heather Lake, General Grant Grove, Mineral King sub-alpine meadows, Tharp's Log, Tunnel Log and Crystal Cave.
Location: Three Rivers
Phone: (209) 565-3134

❸ INYO NATIONAL FOREST

Includes 1,100 miles of trails and six wilderness areas. Main attractions are the Devil's Postpile National Monument, the Ancient Bristlecone Pine Forest (home to the oldest living trees on earth), Mono Basin National Forest Scenic Area, John Muir Wilderness (California's largest), Mammoth Lakes Resort Area, and Mount Whitney, the highest mountain in the lower 48 states.
Location: Bishop
Phone: (619) 873-2428

❹ CALAVERAS BIG TREES STATE PARK

6,000-acre park encompasses groves of giant sequoias. Visitor's center highlights local nature and history. 128 summer campsites are available.
Location: Arnold
Phone: (209) 795-2334

❺ DESOLATION WILDERNESS AREA

Popular wilderness destination has over 50 lakes and 100 miles of trails. Encompasses over 63,000 acres of mountainous terrain.
Location: Near South Lake Tahoe
Phone: (916) 573-2600

❻ MONO LAKE STATE RESERVE

A sanctuary for one million migrating birds, the lake is more noted for the spire-like, calcium-carbonate tufas rising above the water and dotting the shoreline.
Location: Near Lee Vining
Phone: (619) 647-6331

❼ EMERALD BAY STATE PARK

Located on the southwest corner of Lake Tahoe – the world's largest alpine lake – it features some of the most photographed scenery in the area. The mountain vistas and remarkably clear, jewel-like waters are truly breathtaking.
Location: Near South Lake Tahoe
Phone: (916) 525-7277

Museums/Sanctuaries

❽ LAKE TAHOE VISITORS CENTER

Self-guided trails through marshes, forests and meadows provide insight into the local natural history. Underwater viewing tank offers visitors a glimpse of stream life including migrating trout (in season) and the occasional beaver.
Location: Near South Lake Tahoe
Phone: (916) 573-2674 - June-Sept.

CENTRAL COAST

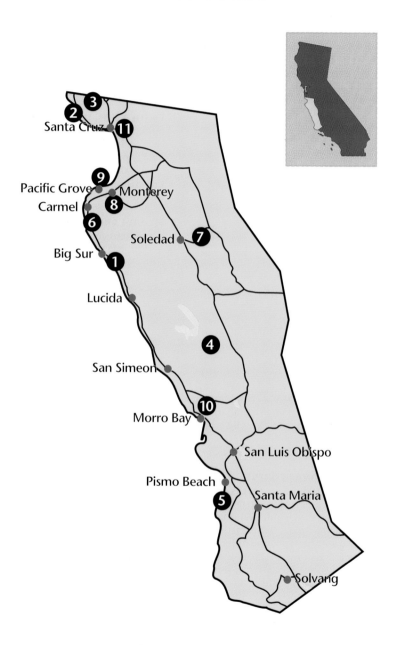

Santa Cruz
Pacific Grove
Monterey
Carmel
Soledad
Big Sur
Lucida
San Simeon
Morro Bay
San Luis Obispo
Pismo Beach
Santa Maria
Solvang

Parks/Wildlife Areas

❶ JULIA PFEIFFER BURNS STATE PARK

3,500-acre park on the rugged Big Sur coastline encompasses some of the area's finest attractions including groves of redwoods, oaks and madrone and a high waterfall that cascades into the ocean. Birds and marine mammals are abundant. The park's offshore area is an underwater reserve.
Location: Big Sur
Phone: (408) 667-2315

❷ AÑO NUEVO STATE RESERVE

A major gathering area for northern elephant seals and sea lions. Huge male elephant seals battle each other for females and territories during breeding season from December to March.
Location: North of Santa Cruz
Phone: (415) 879-0227

❸ BIG BASIN REDWOODS STATE PARK

California's oldest state park features 18,000 acres of old growth redwoods, waterfalls and streams.
Location: North of Santa Cruz
Phone: (408) 338-6132

❹ LAKE SAN ANTONIO

This huge lake is home to southern California's largest population of wintering bald eagles and a herd of more than 400 deer. Excellent birding opportunities.
Location: South of King City
Phone: (805) 472-2311

❺ NIPOMO DUNES PRESERVE

California's most extensive coastal sand dunes include beach dunes over 500 ft. high (152 m). Abundant land and marine birds.
Location: South of Pismo Beach
Phone: (805) 545-9925

❻ POINT LOBOS STATE RESERVE

550-acre reserve is noted for its populations of seabirds, sea lions, seals and sea otters and as a viewpoint for observing migrating whales.
Location: South of Carmel
Phone: (408) 624-4909

❼ PINNACLES NATIONAL MONUMENT

Noted for its spire-like rock formations, which are remnants of an ancient volcano
Location: Near Soledad
Phone: (408) 389-4485

Museums/Sanctuaries

❽ MONTEREY BAY AQUARIUM

A world-famous aquarium featuring more than 100 exhibits of Monterey Bay marine life. Highlights include bat ray petting pool, three-storey kelp forest, sea otter tank, touch tide pool and aviary.
Location: Monterey
Phone: (408) 648-4888

❾ PACIFIC GROVE MUSEUM OF NATURAL HISTORY

Changing exhibits highlight the natural history of Monterey County. Extensive bird and rock collections.
Location: Pacific Grove
Phone: (408) 648-3116

❿ MORRO BAY MUSEUM OF NATURAL HISTORY

Exhibits highlight local habitats, ecology, marine life, geology and native Indian history.
Location: Morro Bay
Phone: (805) 772-2694

⓫ SANTA CRUZ MUSEUM OF NATURAL HISTORY

Features numerous displays on fossils, regional plants and animals and local natural history.
Location: Santa Cruz
Phone: (408) 429-3773

SOUTH COAST

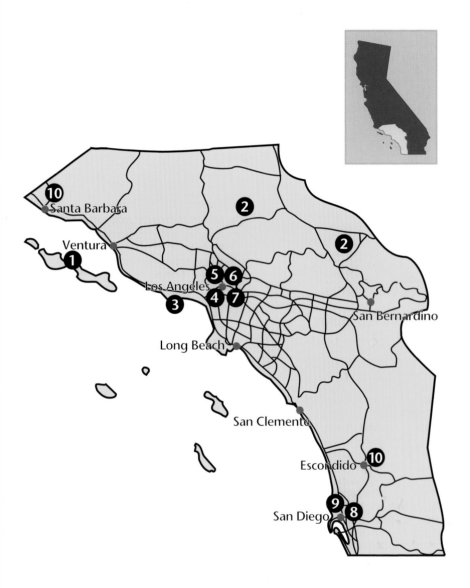

Parks/Wildlife Areas

❶ CHANNEL ISLANDS NATIONAL PARK

A naturalist's paradise, this unique sanctuary encompasses five islands featuring sea stacks, caves, abundant marine animals and sea birds. Boat and plane expeditions depart from Ventura.
Location: Ventura
Phone: (805) 658-5730

❷ ANGELES NATIONAL FOREST

Mountainous preserve encompasses habitats ranging from alpine meadows to deserts. 80 campgrounds and six ski resorts are found within the park boundaries.
Location: North of Arcadia
Phone: (818) 574-5200

❸ SANTA MONICA MOUNTAINS NATIONAL RECREATION AREA

Beaches, rugged mountains and rolling wooded hills are a popular biking and hiking destination. Interpretive programs and guided hikes are offered throughout the year.
Location: Near Los Angeles
Phone: (818) 597-9192

Museums/Sanctuaries

❹ NATURAL HISTORY MUSEUM OF LOS ANGELES COUNTY

Outstanding exhibits on African and American animal habitats, local plants and animals, dinosaurs and geology.
Location: Los Angeles
Phone: (213) 744-3466

❺ GEORGE C. PAGE MUSEUM OF LA BREA DISCOVERIES

Highlights fossils of 200 varieties of plants and animals (including humans) from the million fossils extracted from the adjacent La Brea Tar Pits. Life-size skeletons of sabre-toothed cats and mammoths are among the attractions.
Location: Los Angeles
Phone: (213) 857-6311

❻ LOS ANGELES ARBORETUM

Over 125 acres of local and exotic trees and shrubs. Includes a bird sanctuary and horticultural research center.
Location: Arcadia
Phone: (818) 821-3222

❼ HUNTINGTON BOTANICAL GARDENS

207-acre estate features 14,000 plants from around the world including rare shrubs and trees. Attractions include a rose garden, Japanese garden, Zen rock garden and desert garden. Tours available.
Location: San Marino
Phone: (818) 405-2141

❽ SAN DIEGO ZOO

One of the world's largest and best zoos, it houses 3,400 animals in a 100-acre botanical garden. World-renowned for its exotic and rare species including Chinese pandas.
Location: San Diego
Phone: (619) 234-3153

❾ SEA WORLD

150-acre marine park features a killer whale stadium, avian exhibit, touch tidepool and the world's largest collection of sharks.
Location: San Diego
Phone: (619) 226-3901

❿ SANTA BARBARA MUSEUM OF NATURAL HISTORY

Exhibits highlight local plants, animals, geology, ecology, fossils, marine life, native Indian history and the Channel Islands.
Location: Santa Barbara
Phone: (805) 682-4711

DESERT

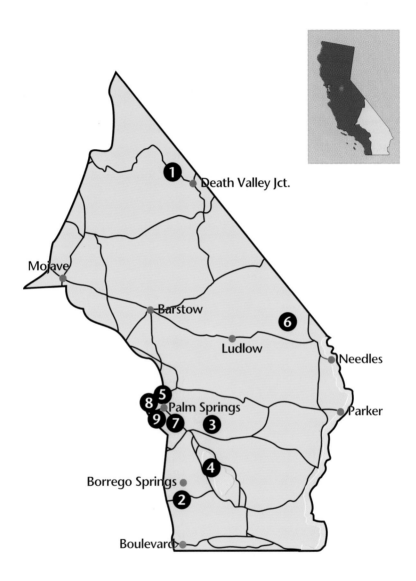

Death Valley Jct.

Mojave

Barstow

Ludlow

Needles

Palm Springs

Parker

Borrego Springs

Boulevard

Parks/Wildlife Areas

❶ DEATH VALLEY NATIONAL PARK

Once the floor of an inland sea, Death Valley is a veritable moonscape with sand dunes, salt flats and volcanic craters. Highlights include Dante's View at 5,474 ft. (1,670 m) above sea level, Badwater at 282 ft. (86 m) below sea level (the lowest point in the U.S.) and ghost town ruins. Abundant desert mammals and reptiles.
Location: Death Valley
Phone: (619) 786-2331

❷ ANZA-BORREGO DESERT STATE PARK

California's largest state park protects over 600,000 acres of badlands, washes, woodlands and mile-high mountains. Abundant wildlife includes more than 60 mammals, 220 birds and 60 reptiles and amphibians.
Location: Near Borrego Springs
Phone: (619) 767-5311

❸ JOSHUA TREE NATIONAL PARK

High desert area with groves of Joshua trees, giant yuccas, spring wildflowers, palm trees, birds, and desert bighorn sheep. Guided walks and hikes in the spring and fall.
Location: Twentynine Palms
Phone: (619) 367-7511

❹ SALTON SEA NATIONAL WILDLIFE REFUGE

One of the world's largest inland seas was created in 1905 when the Colorado river broke through a dike and flooded a saline lake bed for two years. This 37,000 acre refuge of fresh- and saltwater habitats is home to a diverse array of plant and animal life. Nearly 400 bird species have been recorded here.
Location: Northwest of Calipatria
Phone: (619) 393-3052

❺ MOUNT SAN JACINTO STATE PARK

Wilderness area encompasses three craggy peaks over 10,000 ft. high (3,048 m). Alpine forests and meadows can be viewed from an aerial tram that takes passengers 2.5 miles up the mountain.
Location: Palm Springs
Phone: (714) 659-2607

❻ PROVIDENCE MOUNTAINS STATE RECREATION AREA

Scenic park features huge limestone caverns and a large resident bat population. Over 140 bird species and 35 reptiles and amphibians are found here.
Location: East of Barstow
Phone: (619) 389-2303

Museums/Sanctuaries

❼ LIVING DESERT

1,200-acre wildlife park and botanical garden celebrates the beauty and diversity of desert life. Features hundreds of species of exotic desert plants, an aviary, coyote grotto and bighorn sheep habitat. Self-guided trails.
Location: Palm Springs
Phone: (619) 346-5694

❽ MOORTEN'S BOTANICAL GARDEN

Self-guided trails wind through 2,000 species of desert plants. Also features a wildlife feeding area.
Location: Palm Springs
Phone: (619) 327-6555

❾ PALM SPRINGS DESERT MUSEUM

Dioramas and exhibits highlight local natural history, science and western art.
Location: Palm Springs
Phone: (619) 325-0189

CHECKLIST OF CALIFORNIA ANIMALS AND PLANTS

ANIMALS

MAMMALS

❏ Opossum
❏ Ornate Shrew
❏ California Mole
❏ Brazilian Free-tailed Bat
❏ California Myotis
❏ Black-tailed Jackrabbit
❏ Brush Rabbit
❏ Desert Cottontail
❏ Merriam's Chipmunk
❏ Gray Squirrel
❏ California Ground Squirrel
❏ Golden-mantled Ground Squirrel
❏ Flying Squirrel
❏ Yellowbelly Marmot
❏ Beaver
❏ House Mouse
❏ Deer Mouse
❏ California Vole
❏ Norway Rat
❏ Dusky-footed Woodrat
❏ Western Jumping Mouse
❏ Porcupine
❏ Raccoon
❏ Ringtail
❏ Striped Skunk
❏ Spotted Skunk
❏ Long-tailed Weasel
❏ Mink
❏ Badger
❏ Sea Otter
❏ Gray Fox
❏ Coyote
❏ Mountain Lion
❏ Bobcat
❏ Black Bear
❏ Mule Deer
❏ Elk
❏ Bighorn Sheep
❏ California Sea Lion
❏ Harbor Seal
❏ Northern Elephant Seal
❏ Pacific White-sided Dolphin
❏ Common Dolphin
❏ Dall's Porpoise
❏ Finback Whale
❏ Humpback Whale
❏ Gray Whale
❏ Killer Whale

BIRDS

❏ Western Grebe
❏ Pied-billed Grebe
❏ Brown Pelican
❏ Double-crested Cormorant
❏ Great Blue Heron
❏ Snowy Egret
❏ American Bittern
❏ Canada Goose
❏ Snow Goose
❏ Cinnamon Teal
❏ Green-winged Teal
❏ Northern Shoveler
❏ Mallard
❏ American Wigeon
❏ Northern Pintail
❏ White-winged Scoter
❏ Common Merganser
❏ American Coot
❏ California Condor
❏ Turkey Vulture
❏ Northern Harrier
❏ Bald Eagle
❏ Osprey
❏ Red-tailed Hawk
❏ American Kestrel
❏ California Quail
❏ Ring-necked Pheasant
❏ Killdeer
❏ Spotted Sandpiper
❏ Least Sandpiper
❏ Sanderling
❏ Common Snipe
❏ American Avocet

❏ Long-billed Curlew
❏ Black-necked Stilt
❏ Black Oystercatcher
❏ California Gull
❏ Western Gull
❏ Rock Dove
❏ Mourning Dove
❏ Roadrunner
❏ Great Horned Owl
❏ Common Nighthawk
❏ Anna's Hummingbird
❏ Belted Kingfisher
❏ Downy Woodpecker
❏ Acorn Woodpecker
❏ Northern Flicker
❏ Ash-throated Flycatcher
❏ Horned Lark
❏ Violet-green Swallow
❏ Common Crow
❏ Common Raven
❏ Scrub Jay
❏ Steller's Jay
❏ Clark's Nutcracker
❏ White-breasted Nuthatch
❏ House Wren
❏ California Thrasher
❏ Mockingbird
❏ American Robin
❏ Western Bluebird
❏ Cedar Waxwing
❏ Phainopepla
❏ European Starling
❏ Yellow Warbler
❏ Yellow-rumped Warbler
❏ Orange-crowned Warbler
❏ Red-winged Blackbird
❏ Western Meadowlark
❏ Brown-headed Cowbird
❏ Northern Oriole
❏ Western Tanager
❏ Pine Siskin
❏ House Finch
❏ American Goldfinch
❏ Rufous-sided Towhee
❏ Chipping Sparrow
❏ Song Sparrow
❏ Dark-eyed Junco

❏ House Sparrow

REPTILES

❏ Western Pond Turtle
❏ Desert Tortoise
❏ Red-eared Slider
❏ Western Skink
❏ California Whiptail
❏ Side-blotched Lizard
❏ Western Fence Lizard
❏ Southern Alligator lizard
❏ Racer
❏ Common Kingsnake
❏ Western Aquatic Garter Snake
❏ California Red-sided Garter Snake
❏ Pacific Gopher Snake
❏ Western Rattlesnake

AMPHIBIANS

❏ California Newt
❏ California Slender Salamander
❏ California Tiger Salamander
❏ Northwestern Salamander
❏ Pacific Treefrog
❏ Bullfrog
❏ Red-legged Frog
❏ Western Spadefoot Toad
❏ California Toad

FISHES

❏ Pacific Lamprey
❏ Spiny Dogfish
❏ Leopard Shark
❏ Bat Ray
❏ White Sturgeon
❏ Pacific Herring
❏ Northern Anchovy
❏ Chinook Salmon
❏ Coho Salmon
❏ Sockeye Salmon
❏ Chum Salmon
❏ Brook Trout
❏ Golden Trout

❏ Brown Trout
❏ Rainbow Trout
❏ Goldfish
❏ Common Carp
❏ California Roach
❏ Speckled Dace
❏ Golden Shiner
❏ Sacramento Sucker
❏ Pacific Hake
❏ Mosquitofish
❏ Threespine Stickleback
❏ Striped Bass
❏ Largemouth Bass
❏ Bluegill
❏ Black Crappie
❏ Yellowtail
❏ Striped Seaperch
❏ Garibaldi
❏ California Sheephead
❏ California Barracuda
❏ Pacific Mackerel
❏ Pacific Bonito
❏ Black-and-Yellow Rockfish
❏ Vermillion Rockfish
❏ Lingcod
❏ California Halibut

SEASHORE LIFE

❏ Rockweed
❏ Bull Kelp
❏ Sea Palm
❏ Eelgrass
❏ Giant Green Anemone
❏ Brooding Anemone
❏ Moon Jellyfish
❏ Ochre Sea Star
❏ Giant Spined Sea Star
❏ Sand Dollar
❏ Purple Sea Urchin
❏ Gooseneck Barnacle
❏ Acorn Barnacle
❏ Dungeness Crab
❏ Purple Shore Crab
❏ Rough Keyhole Limpet
❏ California Horn Snail
❏ Black Abalone

❏ Black Turban Snail
❏ Native Littleneck Clam
❏ Pacific Oyster
❏ California Mussel
❏ Blue Mussel
❏ Pacific Pink Scallop

PLANTS

TREES AND SHRUBS

❏ California Torreya
❏ Bristlecone Pine
❏ Western White Pine
❏ Sugar Pine
❏ Ponderosa Pine
❏ Singleleaf Pinyon Pine
❏ Lodgepole Pine
❏ Douglas-Fir
❏ White Fir
❏ Giant Sequoia
❏ Redwood
❏ Incense Cedar
❏ Monterey Cypress
❏ California Juniper
❏ Arroyo Willow
❏ Weeping Willow
❏ Lombardy Popular
❏ Fremont Cottonwood
❏ Trembling Aspen
❏ European White Birch
❏ White Alder
❏ California Live Oak
❏ California White Oak
❏ California Black Oak
❏ California Scrub Oak
❏ California Laurel
❏ California Sycamore
❏ Bitter Cherry
❏ Mountain Mahogany
❏ Toyon
❏ Honey Mesquite
❏ Bigleaf Maple
❏ Blueblossom
❏ California Buckeye
❏ Pacific Madrone
❏ Common Manzanita

❏ Coyote Brush
❏ Chamise
❏ California Fan Palm
❏ Coconut Palm
❏ Date Palm
❏ Canary Palm
❏ Joshua Tree
❏ Mohave Yucca
❏ Teddybear Cholla

FLOWERING PLANTS

White

❏ White Trillium
❏ English Daisy
❏ Bindweed
❏ White Virgin's Bower
❏ Desert Lily
❏ Common Ice Plant
❏ Cow Parsnip
❏ White Sweet Clover
❏ White Clover
❏ Pacific Dogwood
❏ Arrowhead
❏ Our Lord's Candle
❏ Elegant Camas
❏ Yarrow
❏ Phlox
❏ Beach Strawberry
❏ Poison Oak

Yellow, Orange & Green

❏ California Poppy
❏ Subalpine Buttercup
❏ Desert Candle
❏ Goldfields
❏ Common Sunflower
❏ Goldenrod
❏ Blazing Star
❏ Woolly Mullein
❏ Common Dandelion
❏ Klamath Weed
❏ Shrubby Cinquefoil
❏ Yellow Violet
❏ Hooker's Evening Primrose
❏ Common Monkey Flower

❏ Creamcups
❏ Rabbitbrush
❏ Tarweed
❏ Barrel Cactus
❏ Great Basin Sagebrush
❏ Common Cattail
❏ Stinging Nettle
❏ Common Plantain

Red & Pink

❏ Skyrocket
❏ Fireweed
❏ Indian Paintbrush
❏ Beavertail Cactus
❏ Farewell-to-Spring
❏ Fringe Cups
❏ Redwood Sorrel
❏ Creeping Thistle
❏ Woods' Rose
❏ Foxglove
❏ California Rhododendron
❏ Red Columbine
❏ Cardinal Flower
❏ Pine Drops
❏ Desert GlobeMallow
❏ Shooting Star
❏ California Fuschia
❏ Striped Coral Root
❏ Bitterroot
❏ Pipsissewa

Blue & Purple

❏ Elegant Brodiaea
❏ Chicory
❏ Fringed Gentian
❏ Showy Mllkweed
❏ Miniature Lupine
❏ Baby Blue Eyes
❏ Common Camas
❏ Mission Bells
❏ Teasel
❏ Blue-eyed Grass
❏ Salsify
❏ Wild Blue Flax
❏ American Vetch

GLOSSARY

Alternate	Spaced singly along the stem.
Anther	The part of the stamen that produces pollen.
Albino	An animal lacking external pigmentation.
Anadromous	Living in salt water, breeding in fresh water.
Annual	A plant which completes its life cycle in one year.
Anterior	Pertaining to the front end.
Aquatic	Living in water.
Ascending	Rising or curving upward.
Barbel	An organ near the mouth of fish used as an organ of taste, touch, or smell.
Berry	A fruit formed a single ovary which is fleshy or pulpy and contains one or many seeds.
Bloom	A whitish powdery or waxy covering.
Brackish	Water that is part freshwater and part saltwater.
Bract	A scale or leaf, usually small.
Branchlet	A twig from which leaves grow.
Boss	A rounded knob between the eyes of some toads.
Burrow	A tunnel excavated and inhabited by an animal.
Carnivorous	Feeding primarily on meat.
Catkins	A caterpillar-like drooping cluster of small flowers.
Cold-blooded	Refers to animals which are unable to regulate their own body temperature. 'Ectotherm' is the preferred term for this characteristic since many 'cold-blooded' species like reptiles are at times able to maintain a warmer body temperature than that of 'warm-blooded' species like mammals.
Conifer	A cone-bearing tree, usually evergreen.
Deciduous	Shedding leaves annually.
Diurnal	Active primarily during the day.
Dorsal	Pertaining to the back or upper surface.
Ecology	The study of the relationships between organisms, and between organisms and their environment.
Estuary	Tidal area where fresh- and saltwater mix, e.g. where a river runs into the ocean.
Flower	Reproductive structure of a plant.
Flower stalk	The stem bearing the flowers.
Fruit	The matured, seed-bearing ovary.
Habitat	The physical area in which organisms live.
Herbivorous	Feeding primarily on vegetation.
Insectivorous	Feeding primarily on insects.

Invertebrate	Animals lacking backbones, e.g., worms, slugs, crustaceans, insects, shellfish.
Larva	Immature forms of an animal which differ from the adult.
Lateral	Located away from the mid line, at or near the sides.
Lobe	A projecting part of a leaf or flower, usually rounded.
Molting	Loss of feathers, hair or skin while renewing plumage, coat or scales.
Nest	A structure built for shelter or insulation.
Nocturnal	Active primarily at night.
Omnivorous	Feeding on both animal and vegetable food.
Ovary	The female sex organ which is the site of egg production and maturation.
Perennial	A plant that lives for several years.
Petal	The colored outer parts of a flower head.
Phase	Coloration other than normal.
Pistil	The central organ of the flower which develops into a fruit.
Pollen	The tiny grains produced in the anthers which contain the male reproductive cells.
Posterior	Pertaining to the rear.
Sepal	The outer, usually green, leaf-like structures that protect the flower bud and are located at the base of an open flower.
Species	A group of interbreeding organisms which are reproductively isolated from other groups.
Speculum	A brightly colored, iridescent patch on the wings of some birds, especially ducks.
Spur	A pointed projection.
Subspecies	A relatively uniform, distinct portion of a species population.
Ungulate	An animal that has hooves.
Ventral	Pertaining to the under or lower surface.
Vertebrate	An animal possessing a backbone.
Warm-blooded	An animal which regulates its blood temperature internally. 'Endotherm' is the preferred term for this characteristic.
Whorl	A circle of leaves or flowers about a stem.
Woolly	Bearing long or matted hairs.

This guide is intended to serve as an introduction to the natural history of California. The following books, most of which were used as references by the author, are recommended for those who would like more detailed and/or comprehensive information about specific areas of study.

FLORA

Brockman, C.F. *Trees of North America.*
Golden Press, New York, N.Y., 1979.

Elias, T.S. *Trees of North America.*
Van Rostrand Reinhold Co., New York, N.Y., 1980.

Little, E.L. *The Audubon Society Field Guide to North American Trees.*
A. Knopf, New York, N.Y., 1979.

Munz, P.A. *A Flora of Southern California.*
University of California Press, Berkeley, CA., 1974.

Ornduff, Robert. *An Introduction to California Plant Life.*
University of California Press, Berkeley, CA., 1974.

Spellenberg, R. *The Audubon Society Field Guide to North American Wildflowers.* A. Knopf, New York, N.Y., 1979.

Venning, D. *Wildflowers of North America.*
Golden Press, New York, N.Y., 1984.

MAMMALS

Burt, W.H., and Grossenheider, R.P. *A Field Guide to the Mammals of America North of Mexico.* Houghton Mifflin, Boston, Mass. 1976.

Halfpenny, J.C. *A Field Guide to Mammal Tracking in North America.*
Johnson Books, Boulder, Colorado, 1986.

Ingles, Lloyd, G. *Mammals of the Pacific States.*
Stanford University Press, Stanford, CA., 1965.

Murie, O.J. *A Field Guide to Animal Tracks.*
Houghton Miflin, Boston, Mass., 1975.

Walker, E.P. *Mammals of the World.*
Johns Hopkins University Press, Baltimore, Maryland, 1975.

Whitaker, J.D. *The Audubon Society Field Guide to North American Mammals.* A. Knopf, New York, N.Y., 1980.

BIRDS

Cogswell, H.L. *Water Birds of California.*
University of California Press, Berkeley, CA, 1977.

Udvardy, M.D.F. *The Audubon Society Field Guide to North American Birds.*
A. Knopf, New York, N.Y., 1977.

Peterson, R.T. *A Field Guide to the Western Birds.*
Houghton Mifflin, Boston, Mass., 1990.

Small, Arnold. *The Birds of California.*
Winchester Press, New York, N.Y., 1974.

REPTILES & AMPHIBIANS

Behler, J.L., and King, F.W. *The Audubon Society Field Guide to North American Reptiles and Amphibians.* A. Knopf, New York, N.Y., 1979.

Stebbins, R.C. *Amphibians and Reptiles of California.* University of California Press, Berkeley, CA., 1972.

Stebbins, R.C. *Amphibians and Reptiles of Western North America.* Houghton Mifflin Co., Boston, Mass., 1985.

Smith, H., and Brodie, E. *Reptiles of North America.* Golden Press, New York, N.Y., 1982.

FISHES

Boschung, H.T. et al *The Audubon Society Field Guide to North American Fishes, Whales and Dolphins.* Alfred Knopf, New York, N.Y., 1989.

Eschemeyer, W.N., and Herald, E.S. *A Field Guide to Pacific Coast Fishes.* Houghton Miflin, Boston, MA., 1983.

Moyler, P.B. *Inland Fishes of California.* University of California Press, Berkeley, CA., 1976.

Page, L.M., and Burr, B.M. *A Field Guide to Freshwater Fishes.* Houghton Miflin, Boston, Mass., 1991.

SEASHORE LIFE

Dawson, E.Y. and Foster, M.S. *Seashore Plants of California.* University of California Press, Berkeley, CA.,1982.

Hinton, Sam. *Seashore Life of California.* University of California Press, Berkeley, CA., 1987.

Rehder, H.A. *The Audubon Society Guide to North American Seashells.* Alfred Knopf, New York, N.Y., 1981.

NATURAL HISTORY

Hall, C.A. Jr. *Natural History of the White-Inyo Range.* University of California Press, Berkeley, CA., 1991.

Henson, P. and Ussner, D.J. *The Natural History of Big Sur.* University of California Press, Berkeley, CA., 1994.

Perry, J. and Perry, J.G. *The Sierra Club Guide to the Natural Areas of California.* Sierra Club Books, San Francisco, CA.,1983.

Schoenherr, A.A., *A Natural History of California.* University of California Press, Berkeley, CA., 1992.

Williams, J.C. and Monroe, H.C. *Natural History of Northern California.* Kendall/Hunt Publishing, Dubuque, Iowa, 1976.

Vessel, M.P. and Wong, H.H. *The Natural History of Vacant Lots.* University of California Press, Berkeley, CA., 1987.

NOTES

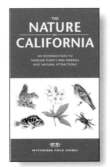
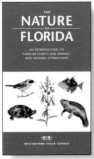

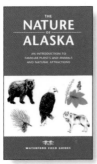